THE
GOD
OF THE
GARDEN

ANDREW PETERSON

THE
GOD
OF THE
GARDEN

Thoughts on Creation, Culture, and the Kingdom

B&H
PUBLISHING
BRENTWOOD, TENNESSEE

978-1-0877-3695-2

Published by B&H Publishing Group
Brentwood, Tennessee

Dewey Decimal Classification: 248.84
Subject Heading: CHRISTIAN LIFE / PRAISE OF GOD /
WORSHIP

Cover design and illustration by Stephen Crotts.
Chapter illustrations by Andrew Peterson.

The William Wordsworth quote at the beginning of
each chapter is taken from the poem, "Ode: Intimations of
Immortality from Recollections of Early Childhood."

Poems by Shigé Clark (pages 139–140) and Pete Peterson
(pages 141–143) are used by permission of the writer.

3 4 5 6 7 8 9 • 27 26 25 24 23

For Art and Janis Peterson

Who impressed on me the words of the Lord, talked
about them when they were sitting in their house,
when they were walking by the way, when they were
lying down and rising up. They also planted trees.

And calling to him a child,
he put him in the midst of them and said,
"Truly, I say to you,
unless you turn and become like children,
you will never enter the kingdom of heaven."
—Matthew 18:2–3 (ESV)

CONTENTS

WELCOME TO
THE CHAPTER HOUSE

The Child is father of the Man;
And I could wish my days to be
Bound each to each by natural piety.

—William Wordsworth

This is a story about place.

It's fitting, then, that the whole of this book was written in one place, surrounded by the same walls, the same smells, the same creaks and quirks and comforts. Because of my job, I've done a lot of traveling, so most of my songs and stories were written in all manner of places: coffeehouses, church fellowship halls, green rooms, airplanes, park benches, and recording studios. I've spent much of the last twenty-five years on the move. Due to COVID-19, early 2020 had me literally and figuratively grounded in a way that allowed me—*forced* me—to work in place: slowly, rhythmically, without the frantic pace to which I had grown accustomed. I had to exercise my imagination, casting thoughts far and wide, thoughts creeping like ivy beyond the confines of this place to other places in the distant past and the distant future, traveling not on an airplane or in a tour bus but in the pages of books and the memories kept by photographs.

Several weeks into the spring lockdown, as Jamie and I drifted off to sleep, I realized that I had spent more consecutive nights in my own bed than I had in more than twenty years. I was so happy. Yes, there were financial concerns;

yes, there was a simmering anxiety brought on by that awful virus; yes, death and tragedy seemed to be ripping the world apart at the seams; yes, there were things we wanted to do but couldn't. But I had never, since 1997 when we moved to Nashville, been home with my bride for every day of spring. I had never witnessed, from home, the way Lent blossomed into Easter. Nor had I ever been present for each heady day of high summer or its withering into the blaze of autumn. Certain birds came to the feeder at certain times. On walks to the lower pasture I came to expect the white flash of rabbits bounding into the brush in certain places. Among the many deer that passed through, one orphaned fawn hung around for weeks, brazenly grazing the patch of corn just beyond our car. I learned to spot box turtles standing frozen in the weeds and eyeing me with their severe yellow irises near the seasonal stream. The field of wildflowers lured butterflies and gold finches. The bees provided fifty pounds of honey. The pear tree produced, at last, exactly one edible pear. We got bowl after bowl of blueberries, raspberries, and strawberries, harvested on dewy mornings as the sun crested the hill. The chickens provided eggs; the raised beds provided kale and onions and cucumbers. And the cottage garden out front, with someone to tend it on a daily basis, exploded with firework displays of tulips, hyacinths, foxgloves, yarrow, coneflowers, delphiniums, catmint, Russian sage, hollyhocks, geraniums, lupines, and asters. The whole of the property seemed to enjoy being cared for by this amateur gardener tromping about. It responded favorably to me, and I to it. In short, I had never been so intimately connected to Place—to *this* place we call The Warren, utterly unique in all the wide world.

When we moved here about fourteen years ago, I dreamed that one day I'd find a way to build a little writing cabin. We homeschooled our kids (which really means Jamie home-schooled our kids), so it was difficult to find a quiet place in the house to write. Life was busy and money was tight, so building something was out of the question. I managed by working on books at the local coffeehouse and songs in our living room late at night after everyone else had gone to bed. Of the songs I wrote at home over the years, 99 percent of them were composed between midnight and 4:00 a.m. Then about five years ago, a friend came to visit from out of town. We gave her a tour of the property, and at the end she asked me, "But where do *you* work?" We laughed. I told her that I hoped to build a place someday, but we couldn't afford it. It was clear that her wheels were turning. A few weeks later we got a check in the mail, along with a note that read, "This is for the foundation. Get started."

She knew that if I just took the leap and poured the footers, I'd find a way to finish. She was right. Thanks to the help of several generous people, about a year later I completed construction on this little writing cottage called the Chapter House. I found an old $400 piano on Craigslist and settled it in the corner, and the first day I sat down to work on a song, I bowed my head and cried with thanksgiving. In this place called Nashville there's a place called The Warren. And here at The Warren, just beyond the stone arch and the bed of tulips, there's a place called the Chapter House. That's where every sentence of this book was written.

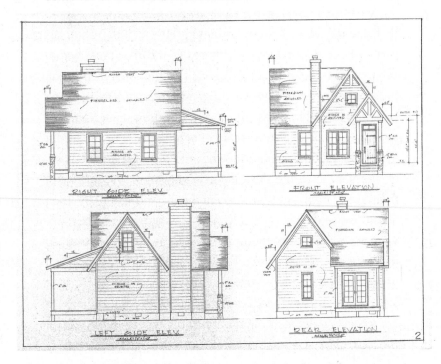

The walls are insulated with books and hung with pictures. There's the painting I picked up in Nome, Alaska. There's the watercolor of St. Francis my son made for me. There on the piano sits the statue of Janner and Kalmar Wingfeather, a gift from my sculptor friend Scott. There's a drawing table in the corner where I sketch trees. Next to the piano, a guitar with elvish inlay hangs on the wall. Below the window is an antique oaken kneeler from England, where I light a candle and pray on my better days. There's not a single day that I don't give thanks to God for this place within a place within a place that I love.

WELCOME TO THE CHAPTER HOUSE

The better part of the Chapter House is made of trees. The ceiling, the floor, the front door, the bookshelves, the drawing table, the mantel, and the pine frame were once living trees. That means something. What also makes a house meaningful is the stories that it houses. Our bodies need a place to live, and the places we live need bodies to inhabit them. Humans were created to care for the world, and the world was created to be cared for. This story about place is framed by trees, but it isn't just about trees. Trees are the framework by which these stories were written and understood—and if not understood, then at least explored. The trunks of several of the big trees here at The Warren bear 2x4 planks which were hammered in by my children, one over another, so they could reach the upper branches. The chapters in this book are like those 2x4s, made of trees and affixed to trees in order to reach the wondrous world of the overstory, and also to get a new and enlightening glimpse of the ground.

Trees need to be still in order to grow. We need to be still in order to see that God's work in us and around us is often slow and quiet, patient and steady. It was in that stillness that I sat here in the Chapter House, watching through its windows as creation cycled through its changes, to delve into the soil of the past, to branch into the air of the present, and to strain toward the skies of the coming Kingdom.

And so it begins with a maple seed caught on a gust of wind, sailing up over the eaves of the Chapter House, past the Cumberland River, clear over the horse pastures of Kentucky, and into the wide plains of central Illinois. The seed pinwheels

TWO MAPLES, A DOGWOOD, AND THE THINKING TREE

There was a time when meadow, grove, and stream,

The earth, and every common sight,

To me did seem

Appareled in celestial light,

The glory and the freshness of a dream.

—William Wordsworth

Two maple trees.

One big and one little.

That's what I remember first about my childhood in Monticello, Illinois. If you were location scouting for a film set in the quaintest, most idyllic version of small-town America, you could do a lot worse than Monticello. There was a town square with a Dairy Queen and a pizza place on the corner. We had fireflies in the summer and snow ploughs in the winter, softball games in the park and bullies on the playground. We even had tornadoes every so often, scouring miles and miles of corn fields, splintering old barns.

Our family lived in the parsonage, a humble house on the church property where the preacher lived rent-free. Looking at the little brick house from State Street, you'd see on its right a field of corn that bordered the side yard and stretched back for a few hundred yards. The cornfield border turned left and enclosed the backyard and the church building, then angled back to the road on the left, beyond the church, hemming us in every summer with a waving wall of green. In the backyard, between the house and the corn, stood the two maple trees: one big, and one little. I don't know if they were planted at different times, or if perhaps one lost its upper limbs in a storm, but I have a hazy memory of referring to those maples as "big" and "little."

There's a good chance I never said it out loud, but all these years and miles away, if I close my eyes and picture Monticello, the first thing I see is those two leafy trees in the foreground of a sea of tall, green corn, corn stretching away forever beneath a vibrant blue dome. Another hazy memory: climbing a wooden ladder into the shadowy boughs to marvel at four sky-blue eggs cradled in their twiggy nest. It was 1980. I was seven.

Corn. Blue sky. Two maples, one big and one little. Those four things encapsulate the greater part of my childhood memory. I never found out who planted those trees, but if I had, I'd thank them. They're as much a part of my history as that little house and the people who lived in it. There's a scene in It's a Wonderful Life where a drunk George Bailey crashes his car into a tree. The owner of the house yells at him and says, "My grandfather planted that tree!" It's a small moment in a big story, but I always loved it. He might as well have said, "I'm rooted to this place. I'm a part of a larger story. I care about things that last, and about things handed down. I care about what grows and gives shade, about creation, and about the broad sweep of the ages." These trees weren't mine, but I wish they had been.

From a distance of forty years, I see that little boy climbing into the maple boughs to look at the eggs and I want to hug him. Even now, my heart swells a little and I clench my jaw to keep from crying for the sadness of what was lost, and lost so soon. Pain was sure to come, but I didn't know it yet.

I recall a passive, almost mindless movement through the days, taking note of moments that strike me now as precious and undefiled, but were taken then as a matter of fact and no less wonderful because of it: a rabbit vanishing into the green shadows cast by the leafy wall of corn, sunlight warming the strawberry patch, the cat giving birth on a pile of laundry, the chattering spill of church members into the bright air of the parking lot after the service on Sunday, the muted walk to Lincoln Elementary School in the hushed world of a snowy morning. That chapter of my childhood cradled a profound innocence, which is why I now find it so baffling that I whole-heartedly invited such sin into my heart one day at school when on Book Day my friend smuggled one of his dad's magazines from home; baffling that first and second grades were spent in abject terror of being called on or even looked at; baffling that the little golden boy I was could be so easily and willingly tarnished.

What happened? Try as I might, I can find nothing in the memory-scape of Monticello to explain it. The summer days gleamed with blue and green and gold, the nights with fire-flies, the winters with moonlit snow. The two maples framed the backyard and offered their shade in June, their glory in October, their stark outlines in February, their russet buds in April. They were benevolent sentinels, watching as the little boy and his siblings slipped into the corn rows, as they chased the cocker spaniel, as they sledded on the snow pile in the parking lot. Always present, rooted to the ground in a way that suggests permanence, the maples were yet always changing, always plunging their roots deeper, stretching their branches higher and broader, fattening their trunks by a ring per year; always swaying in the wind, sprouting, sighing, creaking, boasting in summer and blushing in autumn. I loved those maples. We think of trees as sturdy, immovable obelisks, yet they're fully alive, imbued with motion and growth. Yes, trees stand still. But they also dance. And they break.

———

In 2016 I had a concert in Champaign, Illinois, which is about twenty minutes from Monticello. The good people who promoted the show let me borrow someone's car so I could drive over and reminisce for a few hours before sound check. I was thrilled, hoping that something there would trigger a new memory. Childhood is a photo album of mostly blank pages, and I was hunting for a few Polaroids to restore to their rightful place. Maybe this is a better analogy: childhood is an art museum that's been pillaged by time, and there on the blank walls, below the faint rectangular outline where the painting used to be, hang little plaques that read, "The Source of Your Anxiety," "The Reason You're So Desperate to Be Loved," "The Day You Knew the World Was Broken," and "The Day You Knew You Were Just as Broken as the World."

We journey in pain, and the presence of pain demands an answer. When you stub your toe in the dark, you don't just hop around for a minute and then go to bed—you flip on the light to see what hurt you. True, I wanted to recapture some of the innocent wonder of boyhood in Monticello, a season of my life I've long thought of as a sort of Eden, but there was more to the expedition than that. Maybe I had repressed the truth. I had been hurt, and I wanted to switch on the light to understand what had hurt me. Maybe there was a sinister presence even there in that Edenic little town that had marked me, shaped me, wrecked me, and I had subconsciously taken the paintings off the wall and stowed them in the basement.

I was hunting for nostalgia, yes, but here's another truth: I was afraid of what I might find.

———

I drove west from Champaign under a gray, featureless sky. The stubble of corn stalks in all those wide, muddy fields was all that remained of the harvest a month prior. When I exited the highway for Monticello, I turned off the GPS, determined to find my way without it. Right away, I happened upon the cemetery where my brother and I used to ride our bikes through a hilly forest of gravestones and old trees, where I always felt a thrill of intrigue among all those bones stowed among the roots. I coasted through the town square, where our family sometimes sat on a stone wall in front of the courthouse to eat Dairy Queen ice cream after church. As I drove I couldn't shake the feeling that the town held some secret to understanding my childhood a little better, but I was only getting snippets. I followed the cold, quiet streets past the elementary school, where one wintry afternoon I almost froze to death waiting for my brother to walk me home. He had forgotten to collect me, and I dutifully waited so long I fell asleep on a pile of snow. My parents found me after dark. A chilling memory, if you'll pardon the pun, but not a new one. I finally made my way north, past the library with the bust of the horse out front, past the train museum that commemorates Abe Lincoln's visits to the town before his presidency, then a string of unusually large Gothic Revival houses called "Millionaire's Row," to—there it was!—Monticello Christian Church, and the parsonage where we lived.

It must be different for people who stuck around, whose years of memories overlay each spot. Because we moved when I was seven, the memories are held in time, a series of vignettes frozen in amber. I floated through the tree-lined streets like a ghost, silent and attentive to every detail as an observer rather than as a participant, as if everyone else was going about their business with blinders on and I alone was able to see the town for what it was. But here's the mystery: "what it was" remained veiled even from me, like a word on the tip of my tongue, or the corner piece of a puzzle that eludes discovery.

This is going to sound strange, but when I was a boy, alone in the backyard or the bedroom, I remember whispering to myself, with a shiver of wonder, "I am *me*." I was a Self. Among all the cogs and pistons of the universe, this one little bolt at least was sentient and self-aware, able to form thoughts and to isolate himself as a separate, cognizant being with agency. Of all the things I could choose to think about, whether Tonka trucks, or hide and seek, or the color of the clouds, I occasionally stopped whatever I was doing and willed myself to dwell on my own personhood as a member of the universe. "I . . . am . . . *me*," I would think, and then shiver all over. My brain would crackle. I was particular. Who I was was a Who. Not just a What. And I was a Who who could think about being a Who. And that grown-up Who was now ghosting his way down the streets of Monticello in December, unable to put his finger on the What he was meant to discover.

I parked the car in the gravelly church parking lot, climbed out into the cold prairie wind and looked around. The corn field was gone, replaced by a small development of houses and an expansion of the church property. I spotted a stand of crab apple trees in front of the church, and suddenly remembered eating their bitter fruit after a Sunday night service.

Ah! A new memory, at last. And a good one, at that.

I walked toward the back of the house and looked for my two maples. But there were now several trees, and it was winter, which made it hard to tell which were mine. A couple of them looked equal in size, both rather large, and I wondered if I had invented the part about one being smaller. They were also entirely in the wrong place, which made me wonder if they were the original trees at all. Maples grow up to two feet per year, so one would think that forty years would have been enough for them to dominate the view.

If I had to choose a favorite tree, I suppose it would be the maple, not only because it's attached to my earliest memory of trees, but because there's something inherently pleasing about a maple. In a platonic sense, they are to me the Form of Tree. When a kid draws a tree—a brown trunk with a green, cloudy blob above it—I always assume it's a maple. Not only are they proportionally pleasing, they blaze in autumn, and the crunch of those orange and brown leaves on the lawn conjures images of pumpkins, bonfires, and kids like me in Luke Skywalker outfits on Halloween. A maple can be other-worldly when there's still some incandescent green at the center of the fiery canopy—all the better when viewed from below, on a crisp, cloudless day. An old maple showing off in October is evidence of the delight of God. All that, and they give you syrup, too.

When we moved to The Warren in the summer of 2008, Jamie and I were giddy about the autumnal colors at the turning of the next season. But, alas, nothing much happened. We have a lot of hackberries, whose leaves usually just shrivel and blacken, and most of the other trees on the property are eastern red cedars. They're pretty enough, I suppose, and provide a welcome patch of dark green in the dreary winter, but at the time we weren't interested in the stoutness of dark, wintery green; we wanted the ephemeral glory of autumn. That first October at The Warren, I traipsed through the brushy woods, looking for any sign of that Illinois color, and discovered to my delight a single small sugar maple on our property, glowing bashfully among a crush of privet. It was just a little taller than I was. Sugar maples are native to this part of Tennessee, but the invasive brush (looking at you, privet and bush honeysuckle) has choked them out. How did this one lucky seed manage to helicopter down to find purchase, germinate, and then fight its way up and out in defiance of the brush? I soon took my vengeful chainsaw to the privet and cleared a space around the maple, giving its branches room to breathe. That was thirteen years ago, and now it's at least twenty feet tall. The trunk is still only about four inches in diameter, so it'll be twenty more years before I can tap it and slurp up its sap on my pancakes. I'll be sixty-six. I'm happy to wait.

There's an old Chinese proverb that says, "The best time to plant a tree is twenty years ago; the second-best time is now." I've walked through maple groves in Vermont with envy in my heart because it takes generations to get maples that big. Every tree up there, it seemed, was tapped and hung with a bucket to catch the watery sap. If I can keep my chainsaw going, maybe I'll live to see the maples return to The Warren.

But these backyard maples in Monticello didn't seem all that old. I looked around again, feeling both disappointed and confused. What *did* I remember? There was the spot where the strawberry patch used to be; I saw where a hutch once housed our pet bunny, Henry, whom I found dead one morning; that's where the dirt pile used to be, where I played with my toy John Deere tractor. But none of the *things* were there. Just empty spaces. Other than the house, everything I remembered was either in the wrong place or was gone—including the corn—and, sadly, the jury was out regarding the big and little maples. I couldn't be sure if they were the same trees. It was a little depressing, to be honest.

Then another new memory rose to the surface: the skeleton of a cat underneath a sewer grate in the front yard. My brother and I had found it lying there in the shadows one summer day, and it was like unearthing a tyrannosaurus rex. I remember wondering how it died, how long it had been there, whether it had been someone's pet. I think we touched it. I cast a surly glance at the maples which had so disappointed me, thrust my cold hands into my coat pockets, and walked back to the street, following the sidewalk south, looking for the grate. I knew the skeleton would be long gone, but maybe the grate would jog a new memory. Alas, there was no grate. Not even anything grate-like. But I was confounded, because I could still picture it in my head. How was it that I could so vividly recall something that simply wasn't there at all? Was my memory so untrustworthy? A sewer grate isn't the kind of thing that disappears. I didn't know what to think.

"Think."

The word jogged another memory. *The Thinking Tree*. All at once, I saw our family in my mind's eye: all six Petersons, sitting quietly in a circle, our backs against a massive tree trunk. I was squirmy, playing with a blade of grass. I tried to remember more, but that was it. That, and the fact that we called it "The Thinking Tree."

Directly across the street from our house and the church was Forest Preserve Park, a lovely wooded expanse with pavilions and picnic tables and, off to the side, a few softball fields. Softball fields! Another memory: one evening the tornado sirens sounded, filling the stormy gray sky with malice. The multitude of tall corn hissed a warning in the gusty wind. The softball players all ran for cover, and one of them ended up in our house, dripping wet and out of breath in his uniform. We all hunkered in the bathroom, waiting for the storm to pass. I can't remember if there was a tornado, but I remember that he was a stranger who needed shelter, and my parents had welcomed him in.

Somewhere between those softball fields and our house stood the Thinking Tree. I had the faintest memory of feeling excited whenever my parents would announce a visit. Did we actually go there to just think? I gave up on the search for the dead-cat-sewer-grate and crossed State Street to the park. I found a fat, old oak that was big enough to have been the Thinking Tree, as I remembered it. But a quick glance around told me there were several contenders. Oh, how I wished I had known exactly which tree it was. I sat and leaned against the trunk for a little while, shivering in the cold air and the warm memories. It was a good feeling, but I wish I could have been certain. And I still didn't know what we did there as a family.

I texted my dad in Florida and asked him about it.

I don't remember exactly what kind of tree it was, but it was a large one that provided great shade. It was across the street on the south side of the park. I used to retreat to it for some quiet time to ponder and pray. We would sometimes go there to read or share stories. I think of it often and go there in my mind. Your mom enjoyed going to have quiet time. We didn't have a suitable tree on the church property so we adopted that one. I recall that sometimes you wanted to go by yourself and we would caution you about being careful crossing State Street.

At last, there it was.

Not a new memory, necessarily, but new information. A corner piece of the puzzle. On the wall of the art museum of childhood I smiled as I hung a picture of the Thinking Tree next to the plaque that read, "Why I Feel Close to God When I'm Alone in the Woods."

Because my mom and dad modeled it for me.

THE THINKING TREE
MONTICELLO, IL

I stood up and made my way back to the street, intending to cross to my car and move on. I needed to get back for sound check. But I glanced to my right and spotted a for sale sign in front of a creepy-looking house. The windows were dark. Empty bottles and broken furniture were heaped in the side yard, which was overgrown with dead, brown, winter weeds. With a little work, it could be a charming place, and for about three seconds I daydreamed of buying it and moving back to Monticello to live out our retirement years. It was a pleasant, fleeting thought, and when I snapped back to the present I couldn't shake the feeling that the place just looked spooky. I walked over and stood in front of the abandoned house, working hard to remember anything—*anything*—about it, or the people who had lived there. With mounting dread I began to suspect that I had been in the house before. After all, he was our nearest neighbor. Or she. Or they.

Was there some dark secret here? Had I wandered over to the thinking tree one summer day, and then been lured inside—

No.

I couldn't go there. But why would I have no memory of this place, of these people? In a small town like Monticello, my parents would certainly have known their neighbors. I peeked through the front window and saw no furniture, no sign of life. No one lived there anymore. With a furtive look around, I slipped to the back of the house and fought my way through the tall weeds, looking, looking for something that would dislodge a memory and explain my unease. I'm not exaggerating when I say that I was terrified of remembering some traumatic event, and my pulse quickened as I fought back tears. Back in the mental art museum I tried not to imagine a plaque that read, "This Is Why I'm So Screwed Up."

But I couldn't stop hunting.

Then, deep in the weeds of the backyard, I saw several pairs of fence posts set about twenty yards apart, with rusty wires stretched between them. Weeds and bramble choked the ground beneath the wire. Something had been cultivated here. The wind picked up and I heard a slight metallic rattle. A glint caught my eye, and I pushed apart the weeds. A wire marker was stuck in the ground, and attached to it was a little metal label, embossed with letters, like a dog tag.

PAEONIA DAURICA

The wind persisted, as did the rattle. I found another label, then another:

PAEONIA PARNASSICA
CALIFORNIA PEONY

Peonies. Rows and rows of them. The people who lived there bred flowers.

I texted my mom about it.

> That was Mr. and Mrs. Scott Barnes who raised peonies and day lilies on their little farm. It was beautiful in the spring.

Just like that, the dread dissipated, and the sun broke through. They were good neighbors who labored to grow beautiful things, and evidently I would walk over with my family in the spring to see the lovely array of blooms. I have six peony plants in my cottage garden now, and I've always loved them. Time the tidewater sweeps us forward and backward, brightening the man's days with longings he didn't know the source of, and whispering to the little boy that one day he would grow his own glories.

Who knows if I wandered over to the field of blossoms after a long silence at the Thinking Tree? Did kindly Mr. Barnes wave at me in the spring sunshine, clippers in hand, like an archetypal gardener? There may have been a snake in the garden, yes, but it was still a garden. I was so focused on the serpent, I had missed a million bright petals. I experienced a cool splash of relief and stood up straight in what had once been a field of peony blooms the size of softballs and the color of cupcake icing. This house, it turned out, hadn't wounded me. It had given me beauty. I kept one of the labels. It was in my pocket at sound check that day, and whenever I touched it I thought, *There's pain in memory, but there's beauty, too. Going back and digging deep may unearth bones, or it may unearth treasure. Don't be afraid.*

I had gone searching for a corpse, and found a flower.

It was time to go. I walked back across State Street to the car, and noticed in the front yard of the parsonage a lovely, sweeping, dormant dogwood. I made a video call to my dad to show him where I was, and he said, "Hey, I planted that tree!" I walked over and touched it. It sent currents buzzing through my fingertips to my brain, pulsing with time and the slow growth of things and quiet evidences that what we do sometimes lasts longer than we realize.

I hope our property in Nashville is still in the family when my grandchildren are old, and I hope they'll be protective of the trees I planted here, on the off-chance that some George Bailey gets inebriated and smashes into one. I hope the grandchildren climb to inspect the robin's eggs. I hope they have nicknames for the maples. They won't know me, but they'll know I loved trees, and maybe they too will feel the thrum of time when on a cool autumn day they touch a tree that I lovingly put in the ground many years ago. My dad never owned that parsonage in Illinois, but that tree is his. Standing there in the Illinois cold that day, I felt like it was mine, too.

III

SOUTHERN ENTS

But there's a Tree, of many, one,
A single field which I have looked upon,
Both of them speak of something that is gone;
The Pansy at my feet
Doth the same tale repeat:
Whither is fled the visionary gleam?
Where is it now, the glory and the dream?
—William Wordsworth

The maple may be my favorite, but there's another that's a close second, one that I wouldn't try to grow in Tennessee even if I could, because it belongs to the deeper South.

In Lake Butler, Florida, next to the post office in the center of town, there stands a gargantuan live oak (*quercus virginiana*) that's struck awe in me since I first laid my ten-year-old eyes on it. When we left Illinois in 1980 we moved to Florida, where both of my parents had grown up. After a few troubled years in the suburbs of Jacksonville we ended up in Lake Butler, once again in the parsonage, this time right next to the church in the heart of town. It was basically a Deep South version of Monticello—which is to say, if you were location scouting for a film set in an idyllic Mayberry-like Southern town, you could do a lot worse than Lake Butler. Two blocks away from our house, down a long, gradual slope that was the closest thing we had to a hill, was the town's namesake: a shallow, circular lake about a mile across. The water was the color of iced tea (thanks to thousands of years of tannins leached out of Florida's trees), and the swampy borders were populated with cattails, cypress knees, and alligators.

The forests around us were, to my mind, at least, not real forests at all, but rather vast crops of tall, skinny pine trees planted in rows—like corn, but taller and much less beautiful. Of the several species of pines in Florida, the most common is the slash pine (*pinus elliottii*), grown for railroad ties, lumber, and paper pulp. Once in a while when the wind shifted you'd catch the dank odor of the pulp mill just outside of town, and there were always semi-trucks rumbling through town, hauling long stacks of fresh cut pines. Given the odor, the pervasiveness of the ugly (if useful) little trees, and the depressing orderliness of the plantings, I have good reason for my disdain of slash pines. But the live oaks were something else altogether: dark, imposing ents, ancient as the ocean and grizzled as wizards. And there were several of these marvelous old giants keeping watch over the little town. In the late 1800s, famed naturalist John Muir described his first encounter with the "calm, undisturbable grandeur" of Southern live oaks at a Georgia plantation thus:

> *They are the most magnificent planted trees I have ever seen, about fifty feet high and perhaps three or four feet in diameter, with broad spreading leafy heads. The main branches reach out horizontally until they come together over the driveway, embowering it throughout its entire length, while each branch is adorned like a garden with ferns, flowers, grasses, and Dwarf Palmettos.*

On his thousand-mile walk from Indianapolis to Florida, Muir followed the train tracks from Jacksonville, diagonally south to Cedar Key on the Gulf, which meant he would have walked right past Lake Butler. The older I get, the more I realize how special that little town really was.

From our front porch we could see the post office, the library, the jail, the courthouse, the dentist's office, the Western Auto general store, Andrew's Drugs (which boasted a diner), and the Handy Way convenience store. As I said, the lake, along with its accompanying playground and out-of-date skating rink, was a few blocks behind us. I could have hit the funeral home or the barber shop on main street with a well-aimed arrow. On the edge of town, a bike ride away, were Black Angus cattle sweltering in fields, the putter of four wheelers, and swampy sugar cane plantings. In the sense that it was a close-knit rural community, it was quite similar to Monticello, but in every other way it couldn't have been more different. I was a sapling, dug up from the quiet, bucolic fields of small-town Illinois and transplanted to the Deep South, a world where cicadas buzzed, snakes rattled, and ants bit. No bright autumnal maples—just a vast, flat, evergreen forest dominated by skinny pines and live oaks, all festooned with ghostly Spanish moss. I'm sure there were also magnolias and azaleas and a thousand other species, but what I remember most is pines and oaks, like a jungle of Laurels and Hardys—which are both arboreal words, come to think of it.

The live oak at the post office may have seemed to the average passerby like the perfect climbing tree, with its fat boughs draped expansively over the sandy parking lot, but it wasn't true. The regular flow of postal traffic put a damper on the whole thing, since, as everybody knows, solitude is a crucial ingredient in a proper climb. But the real reason that tree didn't welcome me in is that it had already welcomed nests of Florida cockroaches.

If you're not from the South, you should know that bugs get progressively bigger the farther south you drive, so that by the time you cross the Florida state line, the roaches (palmetto bugs, as my mom called them) are obese and sinister, as big and soft as a baby's foot, and as smelly as an old man's. They're shiny, so if they aren't moist, they certainly look it. I've never willingly touched one to find out. And while they were pretty much everywhere in Florida, they especially loved oaks. And the little kids who climbed them. As soon as you fought your way up the massive trunk and got into the first crook, where a pile of brown leaves moldered among the resurrection ferns, you'd skitter back down, screaming and pawing at your neck because you had disturbed a coven of black, shiny demons that stank when you killed them. I've always been terrified of Florida's cockroaches. But I've always loved her oaks.

Since the Europeans came to the New World, live oaks were used for shipbuilding. In fact, the USS *Constitution* got its nickname, "Old Ironsides," because of the way British cannon-balls bounced off her live oak hull. These lovely old trees proved so useful for ships, the Navy established and maintained whole forests of them. One of the oldest live oaks in the United States is on Johns Island, South Carolina. It's called the Angel Oak and is between 400 and 500 years old. I've never seen that one in person, but the pictures are stunning.

I've stood in the presence of another famous one, though, in Thomasville, Georgia, a girthy beast that goes by the appropriate if unimaginative name, "The Big Oak." It dates back to the 1680s. I played a show at First Baptist of Thomasville in 2012, and went on my usual post-soundcheck walk. I happened upon the tree a block away and it stopped me in my tracks. It was enormous. The circumference of the trunk was more than twenty-five feet, and the spread of the branches was more than 150 feet. It exuded an aura of ancientness. The Big Oak had stood there, quietly growing, a living witness to the Civil War, the War of 1812, and even the Revolutionary War; it had stood there in the forest that would become the town of Thomasville back when Bach was writing cello suites and the United Kingdom was formed. And it's still going strong, right across the street from First Baptist Church, where Christian singer-songwriters occasionally perform. I sat in front of it for a long time, just kind of gawking. Later I mentioned it to the folks at the church and they nodded appreciatively, telling me about all the weddings that happen in its shade, about visiting politicians who have posed with it, about all the preservation efforts that have been undertaken over the decades. People care about the Big Oak not merely because it's beautiful, or because it's enormous, or even because it's old. People care because it's alive. Still growing. The mere fact of its aliveness connects those who stand under its shade with everyone who came before. Some mystery of creation yet quickens the *something* that keeps it going, and even though the world is terribly broken, humans still seem to want to be in the presence of an ancient, living witness. Most do, anyway. Some people, unfortunately, couldn't care less.

A few hours from where I grew up lived one of the oldest living things in the world. A bald cypress, nicknamed "The Senator," lived in a swamp for thirty-five hundred years. It was the largest tree east of the Mississippi, and the fifth oldest tree in the world. At an entmoot, the Senator could have regaled the Big Oak of Thomasville with tales of not just the Revolutionary War, but also of the Native Americans who used it as a landmark before the first Europeans knew North America existed. It kept watch over the Florida swamp when Moses led the Israelites out of Egypt. And the Senator would be alive today, but somebody burned it down on January 16, 2012. That person claimed it was an accident, but it happened because she set a trash fire to better see the crystal meth she was smoking. Three-thousand, five-hundred years old, and killed in one night because of a pointless fire. If it makes you feel a tiny bit better, a guy named Marvin had already cloned the tree out of a few fallen branches, and now a reincarnation of the Senator is growing near the entrance to the park. It is fittingly named "The Phoenix."

One of the saddest tree stories I've ever heard was about Prometheus, a Great Basin bristlecone pine in California's Sierra Nevada mountains. A scientist named Donald Currey was using an instrument that allowed him to determine the age of a tree without cutting it down by boring into it and removing a core so the rings could be counted. No one's sure what happened—some say the Prometheus tree was too difficult to bore, other accounts claim Currey broke two of his instruments on the tree—either way, in the end he cut the tree down. When he counted the rings he realized it was 4,862 years old. Then, with what must have been a heart-wrenching thud of regret, this scientist realized he had just killed not the oldest known living organism on earth, but the oldest known living organism in the universe. Think about that for a moment. *The universe.* After weathering the controversy, he went on to have a healthy career, but it's safe to assume he lost quite a bit of sleep over the Prometheus debacle. Once again, there's a glimmer of good news. According to a tree-ring researcher named Tom Harlan, there's another bristlecone pine out there that he dated at 5,062 years. Harlan died in 2013, and never revealed the secret of the tree's location. I don't know about you, but I love knowing that it's out there right now, in the silence of the mountains, quietly doing its thing, bearing witness to the ages.

How old is the oak next to the post office in Lake Butler? I don't have one of those borers the scientists use, and I don't aim to cut it down, so it's hard to say. When I first saw it in 1985 it was magnificent, and judging by the slow growth rate of live oaks, it was there long before the town was. Lake Butler was incorporated in 1859, so it's safe to say people lived there well before that. Thanks to the Library of Congress, I tracked down a map from 1920 that shows First Christian Church, where my dad would one day preach, and to my surprise, the spot where the post office now sits is in a blank square labeled, "PARK." I closed my eyes and imagined the view from the front porch of the parsonage, removing the post office and Andrew's Drugs and zooming back in time to a century ago. I saw a wide lawn,

and the big oak's broad and beautiful arms spread over a gathering of picnickers in their Sunday best. (I also pictured the
cockroaches skittering around in the dead leaves.)

Whenever I think of that tree and what it's witnessed, I
remember my friend Joey, who lived in the house next to the
post office. We were in the same grade, and became friends
mainly because of vicinity. We didn't run in the same circles at
first, but we lived on the same block. We played Ping-Pong for
hours in the church fellowship hall; we played basketball in the
parking lot behind the post office; later, we were in high school
band together; he even ended up being one of the truck drivers
for a tour I was on—all because we lived next door to each
other, in the shade of that live oak. Anytime I went to Joey's,
his dad foisted on me his famous sweet tea, always poured
out of a repurposed milk jug into a plastic tumbler full of ice.

Joey's parents, whom I nicknamed "Mr. and Mrs. Joey's-Mom-and-Dad," were two of the kindest, most hospitable people I ever knew. They were the Lake Butler version of Mr. and Mrs. Beaver in the Narnia books. Joey's mom worked at the prison (as did my own mother), and his dad stayed at home because he only had one arm, having lost his other in a machinery accident when he was a kid. Joey's parents adored Joey's friends, and I was lucky enough to be one of them. No matter how tired they were, no matter what else they had been doing, when we showed up they treated us kids like royalty. Joey's dad would bustle me in and, with a surprising deftness, fling open the fridge, uncap the milk jug, break the ice out of the ice tray, and fill a glass with his elixir—all with one arm. It was impossible to decline the tea; they wouldn't hear of it. It wasn't unusual for me to sit in the cool of the house and visit with his parents, whether Joey was home or not. On Mr. Joey's-dad's good arm he had a tattoo straight out of a cartoon. It was of a heart with an arrow through it, and in the center, in an uneven script, was the name, "Betty." When I asked him about it I said, "Mr. Joey's-dad, who's Betty? Your wife's name is Barbara." He got bashful and said, "Well, son, never get a tattoo when you're drunk and you can't talk right. Back then my girlfriend's name was Debbie."

When I was in ninth grade, I walked under the shady limbs of the live oak to Joey's house to see if he wanted to play Ping-Pong. His dad answered the door and I could tell something was wrong by the way he was swaying and slurring his words. Then I got a whiff of the alcohol on his breath—something I'd never noticed before.

"Joey ain't here, Andrew."

"Oh, okay." I paused. "Are you all right?"

He sniffed. "Joey's sister, our sweet Mary—you didn't know her. She lived in Virginia with her kids. She was killed by a drunk driver this morning." He slowly blinked his watery, bloodshot eyes and wiped his nose. "I don't know where Joey is. When he found out he run off." His hand slipped from the handle and the screen door thumped shut, but I could still see his silhouette. "Do you want some tea?" he slurred. "It's no trouble."

I was only fourteen, so I had no idea what to do. I'm forty-seven now, and I still wouldn't, to be honest. I stammered, "I'm so sorry. I'm so sorry," and then I ran home and called several friends to tell them what had happened and to ask if they'd seen Joey. They hadn't. So I grabbed my bike and went on a hunt for my friend. I found him a few blocks away, in an over-grown lot behind the bank and the old feed store, plodding in the heat like a zombie. We hugged. Soon, several more friends showed up, and we circled him, bikes strewn around us on the ground, and joined him in his grief. It was like a scene in *Stand by Me*. That's all I remember.

After a few weeks, things under the oak went back to normal. The funeral came and went. The grief faded. Joey and I improved our ping pong game. Mr. and Mrs. Joey's-mom-and-dad continued to joyfully host us anytime I and our other friends showed up. One day I found Mr. Joey's-dad on his knees in front of the house, digging with a trowel. His shirt was off. His tattoo was on full display, and his stump was glistening with perspiration.

I approached carefully, once again sensing something was wrong.

"Hey, Andrew!" he said cheerfully, with a hiccup. He had been drinking again. "It's been one year. One year since Mary died." He wiped his brow with his one forearm, then turned back to his work. I saw now that there were pansies blooming everywhere, white and purple petals surrounding the porch like confetti. "Each one of these flowers is for one kind thing Mary did. Ain't they beautiful?"

"Yes sir." Not knowing what else to say, I walked over and put a hand on his bare shoulder. It was slick with sweat. He kept digging. And he forgot to offer me any tea.

Every year after that, Joey would remind me of the anniversary of Mary's death, in case his dad went dark again, and he always did. In all the years I knew that dear family, I never knew Joey's dad to drink—except on that one day each year. He was cheerful as a bird, hardworking, gentle with his hardworking wife, doting over his son. But on that day, he gave himself over to grief and toiled in the flowerbed. By the time I graduated high school and left town, the flowers in the shade of the live oak had grown as thick as a blanket, watered by all the sorrow a father's heart can hold.

If that live oak is three hundred years old, and I bet it is, I'm sure there are other stories it could tell of tragedy, grief, and sorrow that played out beneath its strong, gentle arms. It could tell, too, of the miraculous occasions when those wounds were turned to glory. The other tales are lost to time. But this one happened, and now you know it. Joey's dad died a few years ago, and that house has new tenants. Things look a lot different than they did in the 1980s. Mary's flowers are gone, and the new occupants would be surprised to learn how lovely they were, or why they'd been planted in the first place. But the live oak is still there, right across the street from the post office. If you're ever in Lake Butler, pay it a visit. Raise a glass of sweet tea and say a prayer for Mr. and Mrs. Joey's-mom-and-dad if you do. I fully expect to give him a hug in the New Creation, and he'll hug me back with both arms.

IV

FAMILY TREES

Our birth is but a sleep and a forgetting:
The Soul that rises with us, our life's Star,
Hath had elsewhere its setting,
And cometh from afar:
Not in entire forgetfulness,
And not in utter nakedness,
But trailing clouds of glory do we come
From God, who is our home.

—William Wordsworth

I once destroyed a tree that owed its life, in part, to the remains of my ancestors. Most families claim at least one ancestry nerd, and in my family, I am he. It started a while ago, when I first started visiting Sweden regularly, which led to a decade-long quest to track down my living relatives there. The Swedes are on my dad's side of the family. I didn't know much about my mom's until more recently. It turns out, the Clicks (formerly the Glücks) were French Huguenots.

A quick history lesson, in case, like me, you forgot: in France in the 1600s there was a minority of Protestants, mostly Reformed Calvinists, called Huguenots. They were vastly outnumbered by the Catholics, and suffered severe persecution. In 1685, Louis XIV stripped religious rights from all those Calvinists, who suddenly needed to get out of Dodge. There followed a migration of hundreds of thousands of French Protestants to America, England, Holland, Prussia, and

Germany. My eighth great-grandfather, by the most wonderful name of Bartholomaeus Hyeronimus Glück, packed up himself and his family in Calais, France, and moved just over the border into Germany. In the 1700s his grandson Johannes crossed the Atlantic and settled in Lancaster, Pennsylvania, where they dropped the umlaut, swapped out the G and the U, and became Clicks. The next generation migrated from there to Tennessee to become some of the first non-native settlers in the area. My research revealed that about an hour northeast of Chattanooga, there's an official Click cemetery. In 2015 I was in Chattanooga as the writer-in-residence at Covenant College, teaching a creative writing course for the English majors. With some time to spare one afternoon, I fired up my trusty GPS and set out to find where my great-great-great-great grandfather was buried.

After exiting Interstate 75 I took a left turn at the Hardees in Madisonville, and the world abruptly changed from the modern American blight of strip malls and traffic lights to lush, deep woods interspersed with glimpses of cattle in distant fields, as if I had driven through a time portal. I pushed on for thirty minutes or so, navigating ever-narrowing roads, till the car tires were crunching on gravel and bouncing over potholes. On my right a river was visible now and then through the stands of broadleaf trees, and on the left the forest climbed the steep side of an Appalachian foothill. Once in a while I'd pass a single-wide trailer or an old cabin whose overgrown front yard was strewn with cinderblocks and farming detritus. It was a public road, but in my spotless little rental car I felt like a trespasser. I began to rehearse my story, in case someone asked me what I was up to. "My mom was a Click. Her father's grandfather is buried around here somewhere. Please don't shoot." The GPS indicated that I was all but surrounded by water. The Tennessee River sends out tendrils of distributaries that form long, meandering peninsulas, and it was on one of these narrow fingers of land that I found my ancestors' resting place. Beyond a makeshift metal sign that read "Click Cemetery" lay a weedy patch of ground hemmed in by several tall eastern white pines (*pinus strobus*). I kicked around in the weeds till I found the grave for Henry Jackson Click.

His tombstone was nicer than the rest, made of white marble, like the ones you see in Arlington National Cemetery, because he had ridden as a Tennessee Volunteer in the War of 1812. The picture I found of him shows the rugged, humorless face typical of the early settlers, people who had scratched out difficult lives in what would have been the middle of nowhere. To tell the truth, I was there in the twenty-first century and it was *still* the middle of nowhere. What old Henry wouldn't have given for a sausage biscuit from Hardee's. Supposedly letters exist between Daniel Boone and the Click family, and somewhere not far from the cemetery where I stood, a tree bore the inscription, "D. Boon Cilled a. Bar on tree in year 1760." I don't know how one kills a bear *on* a tree, but Daniel Boone was the man for the job—and it's entirely possible that great-grandpappy Henry would have heard about it.

As I stood there contemplating bears and war and sausage biscuits, I spotted a pine sapling, no higher than my shin, that had sprouted near Henry's grave. With a furtive glance around, I eased it out of the soil and stashed it in the car. As soon as I got back to the college, I wrapped it in wet paper towels for the ride home that night. The next morning I planted it in the front field of The Warren, thinking about what a great story it would make in fifteen years or so. Well, later that summer we got a lot of rain and the grass got away from me. The tree got swallowed up. I didn't realize I had mowed over it until the next day.

Sorry, Grandpappy.

––––––

It wasn't the first tree I had mowed over. Full of good fatherly intentions, I meant to plant a tree at The Warren for each of my kids. I asked each of them what their favorite was, and after a lot of thought Aedan told me, "Red oak." I bought a five-foot tall red oak sapling and lovingly planted it (also in the front field), praying that Aedan would feed on God's Word and grow in righteousness like a tree planted by streams of water. This one lasted a few months, so it was rooted and reaching for the Tennessee sky. But then I got into beekeeping.

Beekeeping is a fascinating enterprise, especially when you're new to it. The bees are so doggone *interesting*, always up to something, whether bearding off the front of the hive on a hot day, or swarming, or meticulously cleaning the hive entrance. I was humming along on the mower, back and forth for at least an hour in the front field, and every time I passed the bees I would stare at them in mute wonder. Well, on one of the passes I stared so hard that when I turned my attention to the yard again I just had time to see the red oak vanish under the front of the mower and spew out from the side in

FAMILY TREES

a thousand finely shredded pieces. I think I paid $50 for that tree. It's long gone now, but the bees are still around, and still just as interesting.

Sorry, Aedan.

———————

Mowing casualties notwithstanding, I'll have you know I've successfully planted quite a few trees here at The Warren:

- two red maples (*acer rubrum*)
- three autumn blaze maples (*acer x freemanii*)
- two sugar maples (*acer saccharum*), transplanted as saplings from my neighbor's woods
- two pin oaks (*quercus palustris*), also transplanted
- two chestnut oaks (*quercus prinus*)
- one white oak (*quercus alba*)
- three weeping willows (*salix babylonica*)
- four apple trees (*malus domestica* "Gala")
- two pears (*pyrus communis* "Bartlett")
- one plum (*prunus institia*)
- one plumcot
- one cottonwood (*populus*)
- one mothernut hickory (*carya tomentosa*)
- five white birches (*betula papyrifera*)
- three peaches (*prunus persica* "Belle of Georgia")

- one river birch (*betula nigra*)
- one eastern redbud (*cercis canadensis*)
- one weeping redbud (*cercis canadensis* "Covey")
- two witch hazels (*hammamelis virginiana*)
- one American linden (*tillia americana*)
- two bald cypresses (*taxodium distichum*)
- one deodar cedar (*cedrus deodara*)
- one black hills spruce (*picea glauca*)
- one black cherry (*prunus serotina*)
- one bing cherry (*prunus avium*)
- one chaste tree (*vitex agnus-castus*)
- two brown turkey figs (*ficus carica*)
- one Kousa dogwood (*cornus kousa*)
- one dogwood (*cornus florida*)

That list was off the top of my head. (In the interest of transparency, I admit I had to look up the Latin names.) There are probably a few more, which I'll remember when I walk the property at dusk. My point is this: I've always loved trees. Whether it was the pine forest where I drove my moped down the sandy back roads of Lake Butler among all those Laurels and Hardys, or the banyan tree I climbed at Thomas Edison's estate in Fort Myers, or the twenty-nine pecan trees at my parents' house, I've made it a habit to notice trees. I'm sure everybody does it, to some degree.

However, living as we do in our air-conditioned homes, working as many of us do in our offices, it has become far too easy to forget how marvelous a tree really is. Even now, looking through the window of the Chapter House in the summer, it's too easy to merely see a green tangle of leaves and branches. But if I stop and consider what I'm actually looking at, the mass diverges into particularity. I see that the heart-shaped leaves of the eastern redbud I planted a few years ago are quivering in a light breeze. I see the long, lazy arm of a winged elm (*ulmus alata*) drooping over the redbud. The corky, irregular hackberry (*celtis occidentalis*) branches twist out over the elm and mingle with those of a leafy, orderly green ash (*fraxinus pennsylvanica*). An eastern red cedar (*juniperus virginiana*) grows straight as a fence post beyond the tangle of elm branches.

Naming helps us to *see*.

I stopped naming chickens a few years ago. When we first got them the kids were little, and back when chicken-raising was novel to us, each chick seemed to have its own personality, which meant the kids took great pleasure in giving each of them names. We had Tigris and Euphrates, Hermione, Toast, two chickens named Larry, Spaceman Spiff, Zebra, and (though they're now embarrassed to admit it) one named Fluffy. Over the years we lost a few to neighborhood dogs and red-tailed hawks, and as the kids grew out of their fascination with hens and I grew weary of investing so much in a bird that could be so easily gobbled, the thrill of naming them lost its luster. It's less traumatic to say, "We lost a chicken today," than to say, "Fluffy got mauled." We only have five now, which is plenty for my egg-sandwich needs, and I don't keep track of any of their names. But it's indisputable that I cared more about the chickens when I could call them something.

My parents named all their animals, too, but they didn't stop there. They also named parts of their property in Florida. There's Goose Grove, and Elderberry Holler, and my dad's home office next to his wood shop, which he smugly named the Word Shop. Naming creation comes as naturally to humans, it seems, as ruining it. Could it be that by naming something, by making it particular, we're making it holy? Isaiah 43: 1 tells us, "I have called you by name; you are mine" (ESV). God chose, out of all the peoples of the earth, the Jews to be *his* people, *his* holy nation, a community set apart to experience his love in a particular way. Calling someone (or something) by name does more than just ascribe affection or underscore belonging—it also adds to the story of creation, places them (or it) squarely in the grand narrative of time. When my parents acquired their six acres in Florida, that land also acquired a name. It became a character in their story.

As I said, before then we mostly lived in parsonages. That model wouldn't be a bad setup except for the fact that the continuation of Dad's job was directly tied to the continuation of his housing (not to mention the hassle of asking the board anytime they wanted to change anything about the house). There was also a marked lack of privacy. My bedroom was literally fifteen feet from the fellowship hall. The house and the church shared a phone line, so anytime someone called to talk to Dad (or the youth minister, or the church secretary) the phone also rang in our kitchen. If we answered and someone needed Brother Art, we had to run over to the church office to tell him. I don't mean to complain, because there were plenty of perks—like the Ping-Pong table, the secondhand clothes closet which we raided for costumes, and the comforting availability of the church piano at 2:00 a.m. when I couldn't sleep. Living in a house that isn't really yours, however, gets old, especially when you harbor a deep-rooted agrarian impulse, which my parents both had in spades.

My mom grew up on a dairy farm in South Florida, and my dad grew up in North Florida, in the town of Lake City. As a result, we had two very different sets of grandparents: the town grandparents and the country grandparents. Granny and Granddaddy Peterson lived in town, small though that town was, and Grandma and Grandpa Click lived in the swampy, Dagobah System-like wilds of Okeechobee, where I always expected to spot Yoda doddering through the wetlands. There were roaches aplenty in Granny Peterson's Lake City (thanks in part to the live oaks, I'm sure), but at Grandma Click's Lakeport there were not only roaches, but also snakes, alligators, fat snails, cows, horses, cattails, barn owls, and rats of unusual size. When I wasn't in fear for my life from giant spiders, I loved it.

As fate would have it, my townie father married a farmer's daughter, and I suspect that for most of their marriage they both longed for a place of their own. But when you become a small-town preacher, you also give up a certain expectation of financial security, and therefore the means to buy property. Still, they always found ways to live close to the land, whether it was in Monticello, surrounded by corn, or in the heart of Lake Butler, surrounded by farmers who often dropped in to deliver baskets of produce and, occasionally, a half a cow

43

from the butcher, frozen and divvied up into various cuts of meat wrapped in white paper. Except for that short stint in Jacksonville, the whole of my youth was spent in the company of farmers.

By the time we three older kids had moved out and my youngest sister, Shauna, was finishing up high school, I got word that Mom and Dad had found an old house, about a mile out of town, that suited them perfectly. I was in college at the time, and Jamie and I drove out to see the place during one visit. Nestled under the light gray boughs of pecan trees on six acres (an extravagant amount of property, it seemed), the century-old house fit my parents like a husk fits a seed. I desperately wanted them to buy it, not just because I was married and already imagining what a lovely place it would be for our future children to visit, but because my parents seemed to grow younger just talking about it. They were giddy. The property boasted kumquat trees, exactly twenty-nine pecans, stands of slash pine, cypress trees with smooth, knobby knees pushing up through the thick layer of russet-colored pine straw humus. There was an old sharecropper's cabin, and two dry wells that were just deep enough to be dangerous. The backyard featured an old rickety corn-crib. The house itself, a "Florida cracker" house, in architectural terms, featured a tin roof and a wraparound porch, not to mention a wood-burning stove and a fireplace.[1]

---

1. The term *cracker* has its roots in Elizabethan England and was used to describe a braggart or a jokester. In Ireland the word craic is still used to mean joking or blabbing. Shakespeare even used it in *King John* Act II: "What cracker is this same that deafs our ears/ With this abundance of superfluous breath?" According to some sources, Brits used the term for colonial backcountry southerners because of their swagger and their penchant for storytelling. By the nineteenth century, "cracker" was

After convincing the elders to let them move, my parents vacated the parsonage and purchased this lovely old cracker house, at which point they promptly went farmer crazy. They restored the old chicken coop and stocked it, built a fence in the side yard to enclose several geese, got a few sheep and a horse, and then started planting. To be clear, it wasn't as if my folks were hipsters suddenly pretending to be country people; rather, it was as if they'd been pretending *not* to be country people for thirty years and now they could let their true colors show.

ANDRES

PECAN AT SHILOH
11/16/20

---

applied to cowboys of Florida, not just because of their reputation for shooting the breeze, but also because they cracked whips to drive cattle. Because of the oppressive heat, the houses in Florida were built off the ground, with large porches and breezeways, and became known as "cracker houses." Now you know.

As I said, it didn't take long for them to start naming stuff. And it started with the property itself. I can't remember what else was in the running, but they landed on "Shiloh," a name we all approved of, not just because it was aesthetically pleasing but because of its meaning. Shiloh, one of the places in the Old Testament where the Ark of the Covenant rested for a while, meant "peace." It was undeniably fitting.

One of my favorite Christmas memories is of driving through the night for ten hours from Nashville while our toddlers slept in the back. Tired to the bone, we cruised through a slumbering downtown Lake Butler, the amber streetlights festooned with garlands and bows, then turned north, into the dark, piney woods where Shiloh waited. My mom had decorated the front picket fence with swooping Christmas lights, and the old house aglow under the glittering stars looked as cozy as a candlelit nativity scene. As we pulled up, "The First Noel," sung by our friend Jill Phillips, happened to float weakly through the static of the not-so-local radio station, so we sat in the Honda for a few extra minutes in the perfection of it all—before we remembered we were exhausted and began the whispery process of unbuckling the sleeping kids. I knew that the near future would include my mom's peanut butter squares, a steaming turkey, the smell of the wood-burning stove, and pleasantly chilly walks around the property. "Shiloh" was certainly the name for the place.

I eventually wrote a song for my folks by the same name, and it ended up on my first record. The guitar part is sufficiently difficult and the key sufficiently high that I seldom play it anymore, but it opens with the lines,

Rickety fence and a rocking chair
The smell of my father's pipe
Cackling goose in the summer air
The garden is green and ripe

When they heard it, my parents gently pointed out that geese don't cackle, and they're right. But "honking goose" doesn't have the same ring to it. That song was also the occasion of the outing of my dad as a pipe smoker—a habit he never would have gotten away with on the front porch of the parsonage, but removed as he was from the center of town, he took it up with gusto and nobody seemed to mind. There's a good chance that right now, as I'm writing these words, he's on the front porch doing his crossword puzzles with his head wreathed in the pleasant aroma of Black Cavendish, while my mom sits in the rocker beside him working on a quilt and trying not to cough. They are delightfully old timey, as is their homestead.

As it turned out, the place indeed became an indelible part of my children's upbringing. Each summer my parents hosted a two-week long "Camp Shiloh" for the whole gaggle of their grandkids. While I harbor complicated and painful memories of my youth in Florida, my kids have nothing but affection for the place. My dad taught them how to skin catfish, my mom taught them how to do crafts. They went foraging for blueberries and sang camp songs. My dad let them hang around his wood shop while he repaired old chairs or lathed pens from fallen pecan limbs. The kids fed sheep and ran in terror from angry geese. They got to know every corner of those six acres, from Elderberry Holler to Goose Grove to the Hobbit Hole under the pecan tree stump, and they grew up unsurprised by the notion that a property would have a name exhumed from the deep earth of the Old Testament. That place is a wonderland for kids, and I've jokingly (and lovingly) referred to it as a sort of backwoods Disney World.

But what about the trees? I'm glad you asked. I've mentioned the pecan, cypress, and pine trees, but not the lemon tree right outside the kitchen window, or the clementine I gave them when I couldn't get it to flourish in a pot at my house. There's a dark, quiet magnolia, standing like a nun in prayer, in the back garden next to the kumquat, and a number of showy crape myrtles, and along the picket fence there's a bouquet of blushing azaleas. An arbor my brother built supports the most effusive tangle of wisteria you can imagine.

But wait, there's more. I haven't told you about the trees my parents planted for the grandkids. I may have mowed down Aedan's red oak at The Warren, but my parents saved the day by planting him a live oak at Shiloh. Asher got an ash tree, of course, grown from a seedling from George Washington Carver's own ash. Skye got her very own magnolia. My nephew Isaac's tree is an American sycamore from a seedling at Gettysburg. His brother Elijah got a Shumard oak. My nieces Elizabeth, Hannah, and Lydia got a Satsuma orange, an olive, and a mimosa, respectively. Because it's Florida, and because my green-thumbed parents planted them, those trees will grow deep and tall and broad for decades, if not centuries, meaningful in a way the rest of the trees are not, purely because of the story of their planting and the children for whom they were planted.

But who will be there to tell it? It grieves me to know that whoever ends up with those six acres fifty years from now will most likely tear down the house and uproot the trees to make room for (the tragedy!) a new and forgettable subdivision or (the horror!) a convenience store. It's unfathomable to me that anyone on earth will care for it the way they have. Shiloh was lovely when my parents acquired it, but in the last two decades the structure and the grounds have been tended and kept by a Son of Adam and a Daughter of Eve who have given themselves to its renewal and flourishing. Everywhere you go, there are signs of my children's presence, in their very own trees, yes, but also in the flower garden where rest the little round concrete pavers in which their pudgy handprints are forever sealed, or in the tree house my folks built them, anchored by an old pecan. I didn't grow up there, but in a very real sense my children did. My parents did, too. The little boy and girl living deep in the bones of my parents came alive there as they cut trails through the pine woods, named the fields, and painted those names onto weathered slats affixed to fence-posts, arranged perennials around the old wells, and strung up the zip line. It's like they were still playing house even as their hair grayed and their joints stiffened. Who they have become is intimately connected to the land they have loved into its own becoming. And now they're old, in their seventies and certainly wondering often what will become of this home they've made. Their children all moved away—to Nashville, Louisville, and Atlanta—and no one's in a position to drop everything and pick up where Mom and Dad left off. But that doesn't stop them. The lushness of the place is fleeting, and all the more precious for it. How marvelous it is to work to sustain the beauty of something even when you suspect, with good reason, that its beauty will fade as soon as you take your hand from the plough. But there's good reason to believe our delights will delight those who come after.

By a stroke of good fortune, while I was working on this book a family member posted my dad's mom's 2001 obituary on Facebook. Granny Peterson lived in Lake City, Florida, just a few miles up the road from Lake Butler, and though I knew her pretty well I had no idea she also had an affinity for trees. The obituary read, "As a member of the Garden Club, Peterson worked tirelessly on beautification and preservation efforts for the city. When Duval Street was being widened, she fought to save seventy-five old-growth trees. Although she lost the battle, she was able to save many of the old azaleas that lined the street, moving more than one hundred to other parts of the city [and] organized tree plantings at schools around the county. The efforts of Bea Peterson's work . . . are seen throughout Lake City each spring as the camelias and azaleas bloom along the streets and in public parks around town."

My dad, it turns out, watched his mother advocate for trees, and I in turn watched him and my mother transform Shiloh into a garden—a garden where my own children played under their very own arbors. My children watched me dig holes and place the saplings in the earth. They helped me mulch them and saw me admire them as they grew. I think Granny would be pleased. She may not have saved the old growth trees on Duval Street, but she's responsible in ways I didn't even realize for the linden tree I planted in the wildflower meadow two years ago. Our loves are handed down quietly.

With each visit to Shiloh I'm confronted with two realities: the Garden and the Fall. Shiloh, to me, is the best of what can happen when humans root themselves to a place. Not only does the place grow better, the humans do, too. When I wander the property, Eden's voice rises from a whisper to a song, and it's easier to see what we were meant for: to love the world as God does, shaping it to reflect what was in the beginning, and, in even greater glory, what will be in the end. But the knowledge that the memories that drape the limbs like Spanish moss will be lost to time, forgotten like native songs, overgrown with weeds or wrecked by the willful ignorance of progress, fills me with a terrible grief. What will become of my mother's gardens, where her hands—hands that carry the DNA of that Protestant Frenchman, Hyeronimus Glück— plunge into the dirt to plant hydrangeas? What will become of my father's woodshop, where with a pipe between his teeth he happily turns candlesticks on the lathe? When my children are old, will they take their grandchildren to Shiloh to eat the fruit of the trees my parents put in the ground? It's possible, I suppose, but I doubt it. Someone else will buy the place. We'll lose our connection to it. The great sadness of Time will bull-doze it beyond recollection.

And here is where faith strides into the scene, clothed with vitality, to remind us of the hope it plants and the love it grows. I have faith that there is a resurrection coming, and our present sufferings are nothing to the glory that will be revealed in us. If our stories are a part of us, then it follows that they too will be resurrected. I don't know if some redeemed Shiloh will occupy that little corner of Florida, but I believe this: in some sense we're all living in a parsonage, longing for a true home. And in the same way Art and Janis Peterson grew younger as they poured their love into Shiloh and fashioned a garden, we priests of the New Creation will be clothed immortal to reign over our own gardens, and we'll do it without the specter of Death hovering over it all, taunting us with the sorrow of Time and the lie of futility. Glory be to God, Time itself will be redeemed, because it will no longer be an adversary, but a friend, an everlasting Sabbath, an unending feast.

If my mom and dad made Shiloh new in thirty years, think what they'll do with a million.

V

DIGGING IN

The Youth, who daily farther from the east
Must travel, still is Nature's Priest,
And by the vision splendid
Is on his way attended.
—William Wordsworth

Moving to The Warren was one of the single best decisions our family ever made. It was the answer to longings we didn't even know we had, and it shaped our lives in a way that makes it hard to imagine what life was like before. It has become an extension of us. Yes, a part of the significance is the community—neighbors, new friends, new opportunities for hospitality since we have more space—but there's more to it than that. There's the contour of the land: the slope of the hill between the house and my office, which required the building and mortaring of stone steps and the puzzle stacking of irregular limestone rocks for a retaining wall; the nearness of Mill Creek, which means that some mornings I can sit on my front porch and see the valley submerged in a cool mist that gives the hills a dreamlike pallor—and it is because of Mill Creek that the land descends at all. The creek is fed not just by springs upstream but by the millions of gallons of rain bulleting from storm clouds, slipping down past our house in runnels to the stream in Warren Wood, and then rushing to join the sudden rapids of the creek in flood, occasionally leaping the banks and submerging local roads in muddy water.

There's also the steep climb to the crest of the neighbor's hill above us, a grassy down where we have often gathered as a family to watch the sunset. The very mold of the earth affects the minutes of our days here. And in addition to the land's shape there's the land's quiet demand that we shape it: the planting and sowing and tilling, the demarcation of garden from yard, of glade from field, of meadow from footpath, all of which alters the shape of our time here.

Like my parents, Jamie and I spent years living in houses that weren't ours. We were still in college when we got married, so our first place was married-student housing on campus. After graduation we made the big move to Nashville and found ourselves in a little duplex in Antioch, a lower-income corner of the city. To my delight, the front yard boasted one medium-sized silver maple. Our apartment was in a cul-de-sac at the end of Faulkner Place, which meant there were kids everywhere, riding bikes or skateboards, sitting on front steps after school, playing ball in the field behind our building. Jamie's a much better person than I am, so her heart went out to all these young people in a way that drove her to action. My heart went out, too, but I was too busy writing songs and waiting tables at the Olive Garden to have much extra bandwidth.

"We should have a Bible study for these kids," she said one day.

I answered, "Sure, that would be great," and went back to my guitar playing.

Next thing you know, she had invited four or five of those kids over on a Wednesday night so we could tell them about Jesus. Eventually we had eighteen regulars crammed into the living room of our little duplex. They became such a part of our lives that our church even sent a van over to our cul-de-sac to shuttle them to services on Sunday mornings. We loved those kids. We snapped photos of them holding newborn Aedan when we got home from the hospital, we took them to movies, and once I even brought a few on the road to run the merchandise table. Twenty years later we still keep in touch.

It wasn't exactly what you'd call a safe neighborhood; we knew there were gangs in Antioch, so I was more indignant than surprised the night I yelled from our bedroom window, through the boughs of the silver maple, at a guy who was in the process of stealing the CD player from our car. The fact that he merely yelled back and continued his burgling was the most troubling part. He didn't seem worried about getting caught, and lackadaisically carried on until the getaway car arrived—which unfortunately was before the police.

Not long after that, we got our neighbors to babysit Aedan so we could go to a movie. By that time, Jamie was pregnant with Asher. We got home around midnight, and I stood on our front stoop, under the shadow of the maple, and watched as Jamie crossed the street with our firstborn son in her arms. That was when we saw the headlights of a car, then heard the explosion of two gunshots. The car sped away. My first thought was one of denial, that it was surely the car backfiring. I'll never forget the terror I felt watching my pregnant wife running toward me with our six-month-old baby in her arms. Our neighbors' bedroom lights turned on in rapid succession and soon many had congregated outside, confirming that the sound was indeed gunshots. We called 911, and found out later that the shooter was a gang member firing not at Jamie, but at the parked car of a neighbor kid in a rival gang. Still, it shook us up, what with our one baby and another on the way, and I'm not ashamed to admit that I began to think about moving.

About a month later, just after dinner, a fight broke out in a neighbor's front yard, complete with death threats and brandished weapons. We hid in our bedroom and called 911 again, talked to the cops when they arrived, then went for a drive to clear our heads. We found ourselves at Target, walking the aisles with Aedan in a stroller as we debated whether or not it was time to leave for good.

When we returned home that evening, we got Aedan to sleep then sat on the couch discussing whether or not it made sense to stick around, especially with the prospect of my regular trips out of town for concerts. We just didn't know what to do, and we prayed for God to give us direction. All of a sudden someone banged urgently on our front door. I panicked, assuming it was the neighbor who had gotten in the fight, demanding to know why we had reported him to the police. I carefully opened the door and was both relieved and distressed to find that it wasn't that neighbor, but another one—a single mom across the street—who had just returned home from choir practice to discover that her duplex had been ransacked by thieves. All their Christmas presents had been stolen, their television was gone, and to add insult to injury, even their telephones had been torn from the walls. I walked her back to the house to make sure the thieves were gone, and waited with her until the police arrived in our cul-de-sac for the second time that night.

Well, that was the confirmation I was looking for. I wasted no time calling a friend who lived about an hour from Nashville, in a quaint little bump in the road called Watertown. I asked him if he would dig around for any rental houses in the country. The next day he called to report success: a tiny farmhouse on forty acres. Forty acres! The rent was $500 per month—which happened to be $50 cheaper than our digs in Antioch.

To this day, I feel conflicted about our decision to move. After all, those kids in the neighborhood didn't have that option. They were stuck there, unable to escape the gang culture, the occasional drive-by shootings, the regular sound of sirens in the night. By moving out to Watertown, we were not only ending the weekly Bible study, but also effectively ending our relationship with them, because it was a relationship born of proximity. Still, none of my misgivings overcame the awful memory of sweet Jamie's pregnant body running toward me with Aedan in her arms, while gunshots shattered the silence.

So with heavy hearts, we uprooted.

———

Watertown was magical. Our house sat on a hill overlooking fields of cattle. A railway wound through the distant hills, and when I sat on the front porch and caught sight of the train rumbling between the trees, it felt like we lived in a picture book. We could walk down the hill and into the town square for lunch at the local sandwich shop. I often biked to the post office with my backpack stuffed with CD orders to be mailed. Our nearest neighbor was a widow named Vivian, whose cows munched grass not twenty yards from our bedroom window and sometimes woke us with their lowing. We were convinced that we had found a Tennessee version of paradise. For about a week, that is.

The landlord had given us permission to paint over the outdated wallpaper, so Jamie and I spent one afternoon rolling the walls and reveling in our good fortune while Aedan lay on the floor and guzzled a bottle of formula. We glanced out the front window and saw a News Channel 4 van parked at the at the end of our gravel driveway.

"What in the world?" I said, placing the paintbrush in the tray and wiping my hands on my shirt. Behind the ramshackle house across the street, a column of black smoke billowed skyward, so I walked down the hill to where a crowd was gathering around the news van. I saw my landlord and asked him what was up.

"Well, I haven't told you about the neighbors. I call them 'The Fools.' A few years back, they started a cult, convinced everybody to sell all their earthly possessions, and moved to Texas to wait for the Second Coming. When it didn't happen," he said with a shrug, "they came back here, at which point it became clear to the other cult members that they were the only ones who hadn't sold their house. It got ugly. Anyway, one of the Fools lived in a trailer behind the house, and," he pointed at the smoke, "evidently he decided to shed his earthly coil and set himself on fire."

If that's not a disturbing story, I don't know what is.

So Jamie and I found ourselves in Watertown, having escaped one kind of violence only to encounter another. During our time there, the Fools mostly kept to themselves, but we did have a few encounters. One of my running shoes went missing from our porch, so I nervously walked over to ask if they'd seen it. The woman grunted, went inside, and came out a minute later with my shoe. "Dog musta took it," she said mysteriously, which didn't do much to explain why it was inside. I thanked her, she grunted again as the screen door slammed shut, and that was that. A few months later I looked out the window and saw four police cars lining the road in front of their house. The officers' guns were drawn and they were hiding behind the cars, one of them shouting orders through a megaphone. Mrs. Fool was waving a rifle at them and I heard a lot of shouting, but no shots were fired.

Crazy neighbors aside, we had a great year in Watertown. Asher was born that Christmas, brought home from the hospital in a bright red stocking. At first, friends regularly drove out from Nashville to spend the night in the country, which was really just their excuse to stay up all night playing Goldeneye on my Nintendo 64. I took long walks through the stands of eastern red cedar at the top of the hill, and went on long bike rides through the valleys. One of the regular routes took me past the Goat House, as we called it, which was an ancient abandoned farmhouse full of—you guessed it—goats. There must have been twenty of them, standing on the porch or looking through the windows like they owned the place.

For a while, we made the weekly one-hour drive back to Nashville for church, but that got old. We tried to find a church in Watertown, but our options were limited and we never settled in. By the time we'd been there a year our friends had stopped coming to visit. And, because we were sixty miles away, people gradually stopped inviting us to things in town. As beautiful and bucolic as the place was, we were lonely. Not only that, we knew our landlord would never sell, so we were still in what amounted to a parsonage.

This whole time, I was a touring singer-songwriter. We made my first label record, *Carried Along*, during our Watertown year, which meant driving ninety minutes to and from the studio in Franklin, almost every day, for months. The photo shoot for that album was in the empty, decrepit second floor of the Watertown bank, right there on the square, and the album cover was a picture of our hammock in the backyard, strung between two hackberries. The photographer was the legendary Michael Wilson, who not only takes those marvelous black-and-white pictures for Lyle Lovett's covers, but who also shot the iconic Rich Mullins photos for his album A *Liturgy, a Legacy, and a Ragamuffin Band*. Among the friends who used to trek their way to Watertown to crash at the house were Keith Bordeaux, Michael Aukofer, and Eric Hauk—also known as the Kid Brothers of St. Frank, Rich's unofficial spiritual order. They were happy times. But as I said, after a while we were lonely. It was a place, but it wasn't *our* place. And without a church family, we knew something was missing.

The lesson we learned was this: no matter how beautiful your spot in the world is, without community it doesn't really work. Even Wendell Berry, who thrives in Middle-of-Nowhere, Kentucky, does so because it's not the middle of nowhere to him. Berrys have farmed there for five generations. His family roots are deep in the earth, and he owns his land. As much as I loved Watertown, it was only an in-between place. In hindsight it's clear that I was chasing a Tennessee version of Monticello and Lake Butler, but I soon had to admit to myself that I was doing it without a true commitment to the community, or to the land.

I offer this as proof: I didn't plant a single tree.

Our church back in Nashville—the one that sent a van to our cul-de-sac every week to pick up the neighborhood kids—was called First Christian Church. The building was a huge brick complex on Franklin Road, right next to Overton High School. The church parsonage was tucked into the hackberry trees at the rear of the grounds, in the shadow of the Franklin Road Academy football field. Since the pastor already had his own house, the parsonage was empty, and they graciously allowed us to rent it. So we said goodbye to Watertown after a year and moved back to Nashville, where I found myself living, once again, in a church parsonage. Oh, the irony.

I won't bore you with the details, but we were there for about a year, grateful but still feeling unmoored, before we took the leap and bought our first house. (Incidentally, a few years later, First Christian changed its name and sold the property to Franklin Road Academy, who repurposed the church and promptly bulldozed the parsonage—no great loss, because I'm pretty sure it was haunted.)

All this time I had harbored a bone-deep longing to belong somewhere, to live in a place that I could work and keep for the rest of my life. And when we finally moved into our subdivision house on Harbor Lights Drive, I thought I had found it. For about a week, that is.

No, there were no crazy cult people living next door. No, there were no drive-by shootings. Though I couldn't have explained why, I knew without a doubt that the house, as sturdy and American Dream-like as it was, was not our long-term home. Still, I planted a maple in the backyard and one in the front, in honor of the big and little maples in Monticello. I also planted a dwarf peach below the front porch and was delighted when it bore actual fruit. Most importantly, it was in that house that I read *Jayber Crow*, a book that changed my life. I've written elsewhere about that book, but it bears repeating: other than Tolkien and Lewis, no writer had ever awakened longing in me like Wendell Berry. By the end of the story, Jayber is a middle-aged man who loves a patch of old growth forest, nicknamed "The Nest Egg." Here's how Jayber describes it:

> There were some double-trunked white oaks, big ones, and so there must have been some cutting in there, a long time ago, but only in a few spots. Other places, I thought, had never been touched. Trees were standing in the Nest Egg that had been there when D. Boone and the others came hunting through, and when the first old Keiths and Coulters and Rowanberrys came in and settled: oaks and walnuts and tulip poplars that you couldn't reach halfway around with both arms and that went way up without a limb. . . . One of the happinesses and finally the greatest joy of my life on the river was my nearness to the Nest Egg. It was only half a mile or so away. I would go downriver along the road and then turn into the Coulter Branch hollow by a lane so little used as to be almost invisible. It really was just a footpath kept worn by occasional hunters and trespassers (like me) and the wild creatures. . . . For some distance in the cane the path was almost a burrow. And then you stepped out of that confinement into a swale wooded with big water maples and ashes and walnuts and sycamores, a sort of entrance hall, spacious and airy. . . . From this place of entrance, being always careful of the nettles, you could make

> *your way up a low, steep slope into the drier woods,*
> *untroubled by flooding, where the dark trunks went up*
> *so tall, and among them you would see here and there*
> *the silver of beeches or, along the hollows, the sudden*
> *whiteness of sycamores.*[2]

Not long after that passage, Jayber is devastated to learn that the forest is being razed for timber. He sees rumbling bulldozers and hears the growl of chainsaws, and is undone by the destruction in a single day of what had taken centuries to grow—not unlike the ruination of the 3,500-year-old Senator cypress by a careless meth fire. Jayber leaves in a daze and finds an old piece of driftwood to lie beside, and soon he falls asleep under a blanket of terrible grief.

I finished the book one morning and likewise curled up on the floor, without the driftwood but with all of the grief. I sobbed. Oh, how I longed for Eden. How I grieved the razing of this gloried creation in exchange for the perfunctory development of featureless subdivisions. How I longed for those immaculate fields of corn, those bright, breeze-blown maples under the Illinois sky. I longed for a garden of old trees and a silence that spoke of God's good pleasure in the world he made. I thought of the wide, sunlit prairies of my childhood in Illinois, followed by my adolescence in the dark shade of the stormy Florida wild, of shadows that had multiplied in my heart there like a nest of roaches, and wanted desperately to reclaim some vision of what had been lost. Could I give my

---

2. Wendell Berry, *Jayber Crow* (Berkley, CA: Counterpoint Press, 2001), 344–46.

children a better memory? Could that boon to their story help to redeem my own?

Jayber's Nest Egg was more than fiction, more than metaphor; yes, it was a potent glimpse of Eden, but it didn't come by way of an unreachable Narnia or an idealized Shire. Berry's fiction unfolds in non-fictional Kentucky. Places like the Nest Egg actually exist. Maple trees are real, as are walnuts and white oaks and sycamores with their "sudden whiteness." Berry had written of an imaginary world I could actually enter—but I didn't know how to get there from the suburbs. That doesn't mean it can't be done, of course. Glory is always encroaching, even in the meanest urban sprawl. But as for me and my house, after six years it was time to go.

We began, tentatively at first, to search for a home that would last. In our case, the city girl married the country boy (though I love the city, too, as will become clear), so I was gently lobbying for a place that was off the beaten path. And yet, we had learned our lesson from Watertown, so neither of us wanted to be in the sticks. Community was important to us, so we explored East Nashville and even put an offer on a house there before we eventually found a home, of all places, in Cane Ridge, just ten minutes from Antioch. That's right: after bouncing around the Nashville area for ten years, we ended up on some property that's a short drive from that cul-de-sac and the silver maple we left behind all those moves ago, just down the road from where some of those kids we used to teach ended up living with their own families. If you had told me that night the gunshots rang out that in ten years we'd be back in the neighborhood, cutting trails through a thicket under the stands of fat cedars, hackberries, and pin oaks, I wouldn't have believed you.

EASTERN
RED — The
CEDAR Warren
11/10/19

As of this writing, we've been here fourteen years, which happens to be longer than either Jamie or I have ever lived in a house. We finally found a place to love. Life is full of surprises, so there's no way to know for certain, but we intend to stick around.

I offer this as proof: I've planted forty-seven trees—and that's just the ones I haven't accidentally mowed over.

VI

THE COMFORTER HATH FOUND ME HERE

Hence in a season of calm weather
Though inland far we be,
Our Souls have sight of that immortal sea
Which brought us hither,
Can in a moment travel thither,
And see the Children sport upon the shore,
And hear the mighty waters rolling evermore.
—William Wordsworth

I'm writing this in the summer of 2020 while the entire world is in varying degrees of quarantine. Back in March I was on tour in England when it became clear that COVID-19 was going to be an issue. Little did we know as we made our way north from London for a string of ten shows that it would become much more than merely an *issue*—it would destroy millions of lives. Few people had any notion of how bad things would get, so I clung to the hope that our tour would continue.

Because of the terms of the rental car agreement, I was doing all the driving. I didn't mind a bit. For starters, I had the most experience driving a manual transmission on the "wrong" side of the road—but the real reason was that I love to drive in beautiful places. Since the windshield, of course, is the biggest window in the car, you get a front row seat to the landscape unfolding before you, and since you can't look at your phone, your attention is always directed outward.

Bless their hearts, the guys in the band were getting a flurry of texts from friends and family back home, informing them in real-time of the deepening COVID chaos. Between texts, they were scouring the internet for breaking news, growing more stressed by the minute. Meanwhile, I was listening to David Gray and pointing out castles and church steeples and little cottages nestled in the valleys. At the time, I just couldn't imagine things would get as bad as they did. I had shows to play, work to do, and a Kingdom to sing about, so I didn't feel an ounce of panic. Concern, yes, but not panic. I realize now that the guys were justified in their worry, but to be honest, at the time I was a little grumpy that they were missing the English countryside.

I lost a little of my heart to the British Isles several years back. I had been to London a few times and had done the tourist thing. It's a marvelous city, with more layers of history than one can possibly grasp in a lifetime, let alone a quick three-day trip spent mostly on double-decker buses. I spoke with a Brit visiting the States once, and when I informed him that I'd been to England, but never out of London (save a quick bus ride to Oxford), he laughed and said, "That's like me saying I've been to America, but all I've seen is New York City. The real England is *beyond* London." Now that I've seen a fair bit of the island, I'm inclined to agree.

Just minutes out of London, you enter the "green belt," a 1.5-million-acre border of farmland and forest that circles the city. The idea was first proposed in 1935 as a way to prevent urban sprawl, to preserve the countryside, and to prevent neighboring towns from blending into one another. Now most of England's major cities have the protection of green belts. I happen to think the concept is genius, though to be fair it has many detractors who argue that it drives up housing prices and forces commuting, creating more problems than it solves. However, having grown up in a country that itself grew up in the automobile age and is so large nobody has had to think much about limiting sprawl, it's easy to see how precious, and how fragile, their countryside really is. And it's not just the countryside—it's the villages and towns, which can be a mere mile apart and yet maintain their own character and history. Here in the States, we have these suburban developments (if you live here you know exactly what I'm talking about) with the same retailers (Best Buy, Old Navy, TJ Maxx), the same

SHARNBROOK, BEDFORDSHIRE
ENGLAND

restaurants (Olive Garden, Ruby Tuesday's, Chipotle), the same hotels, banks, coffee chains, and shopping malls, the same faux-city that's been slapped onto any old unclaimed bit of real estate outside of town. If you were blindfolded and beamed to one in Boise, Cincinnati, or Gainesville you'd be hard-pressed to have any idea what state you were in, let alone what city. You'd have no real sense of the features of the land, the native trees, or the history underfoot—and there's *so* much history underfoot.

For example, just a few miles from me there's a lovely library that sits beside a spring-fed creek that feeds into the Harpeth River. During its construction in 1997 the workers discovered the remains of a sacred Native American burial ground, complete with forty-eight stone burial boxes—boxes which were used in the 1500s in the Mississippian culture. The county contacted the local Native American council and asked how they wanted to proceed. The council said they didn't want the graves disturbed, but neither did they want any kind of touristy memorial set up, so the answer was a strange, meandering, and wonderfully impractical parking lot. Every time I go there, I think about the fact that the odd islands of grass are covering the remains of members of a thriving community who lived among the trees here. In fact, the remains of native settlements have been found near every body of water in the Nashville area, so every time I walk along Mill Creek my eyes are peeled for arrowheads and my imagination is wide awake—especially when I see a tree old enough to have provided shade for those Native Americans. We certainly have history, but with all the box stores and parking lots we just don't think about it.

Have you ever heard of Cahokia? It was an ancient city on the Mississippi River, on the Illinois side of St. Louis, a thousand years ago. Cahokia was massive, with a grand plaza, ceremonial mounds, and even a network of buildings. Archaeologists estimate that at its peak in 1300 it boasted 40,000 people, which at the time made it a larger city than London. During the construction of the interstate highway in the 1960s, a remarkable discovery was made by a Dr. Warren Wittry. A series of wooden posts were found arranged in huge rings, each one twelve posts larger than the last, and the going theory is that they held some astronomical meaning for the community. The good doctor named the discovery "Woodhenge." I don't know about you, but I'm a little annoyed that I didn't grow up hearing as much about Woodhenge as I did Stonehenge. There were many more Cahokia mounds that might have been researched and preserved, but they were leveled during the construction of St. Louis. Think about that the next time you drive over the Great Big Muddy toward the St. Louis Arch. Granted, there are quite a few Native American archaeological sites around this part of America that *have* been saved from bulldozers, but the impression one gets as a kid is that the natives were few and far between, and they lived in teepees and huddled exclusively in little inconsequential warring tribes. But that's just not true. Cahokia was a *city*. Now large swaths of it are buried under the conjunction of interstates 55, 44, and 70—not to mention the asphalt parking lots of filling stations and shopping malls that look exactly the same in St. Louis as they do in Nashville. We have lost our sense of place, and we've lost it in the name of progress and convenience and profit, at the cost of not just culture and beauty, but also of peoples' lives and their civilization. We lost a respect for creation itself.

The fact that the downtowns of many mid-sized cities are being reclaimed for *people* and not just factories and office buildings is a step in the right direction, but we have a long way to go. To be fair, as a person who travels for a living, I have to admit there's some comfort in the consistency of the areas of sprawl that I'm talking about. Sometimes you just want Chipotle and a cup of coffee, whether you're in Boise, Cincinnati, or Gainesville. But I'd trade that quick and easy comfort any day for the wonder that comes with knowing we're walking in the ancient footsteps of cultures much older than the United States, cultures which, because they didn't have internal combustion engines, had to live in partnership with the geography in which they found themselves. There are some wonderful old cities in America, of course, mostly along the East Coast, cities that predate the automobile and the Industrial Revolution, but the farther west you drive, the more uniform things get. The hammer of progress pounded the land to suit its own needs by carving roads out of hillsides, harvesting forests wholesale, and replacing family farms with agribusiness. Don't get me wrong. I love a lot of things about America. But I've also come to love the narrow roads, the quaint villages, and the timeless farmsteads I've seen in Europe, Scandinavia, and the British Isles.

Back in England, as COVID was spiking, we played Birmingham, then Sheffield, then Manchester, at which point the pandemic situation in the United States had reached a fever pitch (if you'll pardon the phrase). The guys in the band were torn between their commitment to the tour and their greater commitment to families back home, so I finally made a phone call to my intrepid manager, Christie, who arranged to fly them home. After sound check in downtown Manchester, I told them they were off the hook, that I would do the rest of the shows without them for as long as it was appropriate. The way I saw it, as long as the churches wanted me to come, I was going to come (again, this is before any of us realized how bad this virus would be). The ball was in the promoters' court.

I was actually excited about the prospect. I've spent very little time alone on the road, so the adventurer in me was eager to strike out, a troubadour striding into danger with a guitar and a story to tell. The plan was to drop the guys off at the train station in Glasgow, then take the ferry (where I would stand romantically at the rail, staring out like a Viking at the salty spray) across the Irish Sea to Belfast, play shows there for a week (where on my off days I would read Seamus Heaney poetry by a fire in a dimly lit pub), then ferry down to Holyhead, Wales, drive through Snowdonia for a show in Cardiff (where I would sit in front of the castle with my Moleskine journal and make heroic attempts at poetry of my own), and then finish off in London (where, like Sherlock Holmes, I would stroll the foggy, cobblestone streets under a pale moon). I was beginning to like certain parts of this pandemic thing.

When I told the band they were going home, the relief was plain on their faces, and they immediately texted their wives with the good news. We drove north to Scotland the next morning, and, comforted by the knowledge that they were headed home, the guys were free to look up from their phones and out at one of the most picturesque spreads of land in the world. Hulking gray mountains marched up into the clouds. Stone fences snaked their way down into valleys where farmsteads nestled by rushing rivers. Cold sheep dotted the fellsides as in the days of yore. We may have listened to the *Braveheart* soundtrack. I know we listened to Kate Rusby.

My buddy Steph McLeod, the Scottish singer-songwriter with whom we shared the bill that night in Glasgow, gave us a walking tour of Glasgow's regal streets. A humbler city than Edinburgh at first glance, it boasted no Harry Potter-esque castle on a mountain, but its buildings were old and ornate, glistening in the Scottish drizzle. We headed to the old brownstone church for sound check, and while the guys were on stage I ducked into the green room to check in with Christie. She informed me that the U.S. had just announced a ban on travel from the U.K., and that if I didn't get home in forty-eight hours I might not make it home for weeks, if not months. Immediately after that I got a call from friends in Northern Ireland, telling me they'd made the hard but wise decision to cancel my concerts.

Well, that was the clarity I was looking for. I was going home. I felt relief and disappointment in equal measure; on one hand I'd be back in the warm embrace of my family, riding out the virus from the comfort of The Warren, while on the other, I wouldn't get to Viking my way across the Irish Sea or wander the cobbled streets of London to my heart's content.

The show that night in Glasgow was wonderful (as were the others on that tour), and as of this writing it was the last non-virtual concert I've played. The Scots are a rowdy and passionate bunch, and this particular songwriter is always grateful for rowdiness (*after* a song is over, at least). I still had to get the rental car back to London, so the next morning I dropped off the guys at the train station. We unloaded their gear and hugged (something I would have appreciated far more had I known that hugging would soon be banned), and that was that.

All at once, I was alone.

Alone in Scotland, with nowhere to be until my flight out of London the next day. I was overcome with emotion. I confess that I cried as my GPS led me out of Glasgow, and not because of the freedom. It was because of what felt like abandonment.

At the risk of opening a can of worms, I'll let you in on something. At odds with my great love of solitude is my great fear of isolation. Solitude is a choice. Isolation is inflicted. For example, one of my favorite places in the world is right here, in the Chapter House—but only when Jamie's in the house doing her thing, and Skye's on the porch writing a song just loud enough for me to hear her sweet voice once in a while. The boys live nearby, so even if we're not in the same room, it feels like we're all together. The pleasure of solitude is not loneliness, but the nearness of love. When I'm on a ramble on the trails here at The Warren I know my friends are a short drive away, my family is close enough to sneak away from—and to return to at a moment's notice—and on my good days I feel the pleasure of God's overarching presence, like the protective boughs of an old tree. The silence is more like an embrace.

Isolation is finding yourself alone when you don't want to be.

It happens, for me, when I'm expressing an opinion that no one else shares. When people look at me like I'm crazy, my heart rate quickens and the story I tell myself is that I'm cut off from them forever, that there's always been something fundamentally wrong with me and that's now a fact in which we're all in agreement. Isolation is when you reach out to a friend to apologize and they won't answer the phone, sometimes for weeks. At worst, isolation feels like betrayal. At least that's what I tell myself. It means that at first, I'm indignant.

The problem is theirs, I think. From there, it's a hop, skip, and a jump to self-loathing, self-beratement, because soon I believe the problem is *me*, and that, after all, is what I deserve. One of these days I'll write a book about the things that happened that brought about the white-hot fear of isolation, but this is not that book. This is a book about trees.

And because of trees, something changed.

By the time I broke free of the clutch of downtown Glasgow and made it to the hills of lower Scotland I had also broken free of the voices in my head that whispered that my beloved band had jumped ship, that I was utterly alone and always would be, that I would forever be better off playing it safe by removing the risk of abandonment and playing solo shows. Because there's a chance that those guys will read this, let me be clear: they didn't abandon me. I opted to fly them home. They were stuck between a rock and a hard place, and wisely chose their families. It was the right thing. The feeling of isolation and abandonment I described is merely the inner narrative I've battled (and harbored) for most of my adult life—one exploited by the enemy of my heart again and again. But what about the Father of my heart? What's the story he tells me again and again, the counter-narrative of my belovedness?

Ah, that's where this story is going.

By noon, I had been renewed. I talked aloud to God in the car. I thanked him profusely for every dry-stack wall, every shaggy red cow, every bite of the Scottish meat pie I bought at a service area. I thanked him for the curves in the M74 that afforded glimpses of snow on the high, gray fells under heavy cloud, and then for beams of sunlight breaking through and glimmering on the choppy, gray surface of lochs in the valleys. He had transformed the desert of isolation into a forest of solitude, and had given me the gift of presence and thanksgiving.

Thanks to my handy smartphone, I discovered that the Lake District wasn't too far out of the way, so I left the well-traveled road and climbed into England's most dramatic landscape, where the forested feet of the mountains border lakes so perfectly placed, a painter could take the rule of thirds for granted. Everywhere I looked the Golden Ratio gleamed; each vista sang the glory of God. The Lord of Heaven was with me, and I had no fear.

I stopped in the lake town of Keswick, where Jamie and I had spent a wonderful week at the convention the previous summer, and retraced our steps along the waterside, past Coleridge's house, and up to the village proper, where I browsed the used bookshop (and bought an 1893 first edition of George MacDonald's two-volume collected poems). I drove up to the Castlerigg Stone Circle, where 3,000 years ago druids, with no knowledge of the God of Abraham, did their best to honor the obvious holiness of the living mountains that surrounded them.

After Keswick I drove through the village of Grasmere, then revisited Dove Cottage, where Wordsworth lived with his sister. It was there that he sat for hours in the garden he and his sister cultivated to work on many of his greatest poems. I'm no expert on poetry, but over the last fifteen years or so I've come to marvel at its power to change us. As with songwriting, a line of poetry can be a cable between two hearts, sending currents of comfort across a span of hundreds of years. The poets—especially those who wrote in place, *about* place—sometimes leave what songwriter Pierce Pettis called "little envelopes of light" along the path, waiting to be found by the lonely traveler. When Jamie and I visited Dove Cottage with friends the previous summer, the tour guide walked us to the very spots Wordsworth wrote about, and as we stood gazing at the gentle vistas, our guide, with a contagious delight, recited the centuries-old lines. Those lines, threaded across the centuries and tethered to the ground beneath our feet, gave us better eyes to see what was already there. Wordsworth wrote that poetry, art, and even gardening, can "move the affections," when we are "in the midst of the realities of things."

I looked down the slope at the reality of Wordsworth's beloved Grasmere lake, nestled in the valley. It was there that he wrote,

> Sad was I, even to pain deprest,
> Importunate and heavy load!
> The Comforter hath found me here,
> Upon this lonely road.

With the eerie sensation that those words had been written just for me, I pushed on to the long, deep lake of Windermere (is there a lovelier name for a lake?) and found a quiet spot among the trees. Here at Windermere, Wordsworth penned the lines,

> Yet, to this hour, the spot to me is dear,
> With all its foolish pomp. The garden lay
> Upon a slope surrounded by a plain

Of a small bowling-green; beneath us stood
A grove, with gleams of water through the trees
And over the tree-tops.

I saw the gleams of water through the trees and knew again that I wasn't alone—not isolated at all, but present in the mystery of time to Wordsworth himself as I gazed at the grove and the lake and the unaltered shape of the surrounding ridges. Some of these very trees had already been sending out their spring leaves two centuries ago as Wordsworth and Coleridge ambled along the contours of this same shoreline. Those trees and that clear lake assured me that, in the overlay of time and particularity, we are surrounded by a cloud of witnesses to God's abiding presence. We are here and gone, but poems last—sometimes even longer than trees. We can walk among words as surely as we walk among the ancient groves. It was only one o'clock, and already the sense of abandonment that morning seemed silly, replaced in time by time's rhyming with place, particularity, and above all, presence—God's presence with me, and my presence in the world he made.

Give thanks for the lengthening days; a heart can travel far in the brightening of early spring. I had six hours left in my journey, and so much blessed sunlight to burn. On I drove, past Rydal House, where Wordsworth died, remembering with gladness the day I sat in the tea garden there with Jamie and our friends, laughing as I jokingly butchered one of Wordsworth's poems with my abominable cockney accent. I could almost see the four of us, almost hear the laughter. I felt the same comfort of solitude—not isolation—as I do in the quiet of the

Chapter House, knowing that those I love most are within shouting distance.

12/17/20   CHATSWORTH, PEAK DISTRICT
ENGLAND   Andrew

I bade the Lake District farewell and traveled south, closer and closer to London and the end of my gloriously solitary day. Every chance I got, I pulled over at a travel stop to consult my phone, hoping to find a good circular footpath to walk before I was back in the footpath-less land of America (more on that later). It proved difficult, however, because I didn't have a guidebook or, well, a guide. That's when an idea struck. I pulled over and texted my friend Micah, an American ex-pat who lives in Oxford.

Micah! It's Andrew. I'm in England. Can you do some recon for me? I'm on the way to London from the

*Lakes. I have time for exactly one footpath before the
sun sets. Can you find me a good one?*

Micah, a fellow rambler, was happy to oblige.

Give me a few minutes and I'll text you some options.

Next thing you know, I was on my way to Buckley Green.
Micah told me that it was near where Mary Arden grew up—
Mary Arden Shakespeare, that is, the mother of the Bard
himself. When Shakespeare wrote As You Like It, he likely
based the forest on these woodlands—woodlands where, in
the play, the Edenic forest is full of magic, apparitions, and
the discovery of love. The sun was going fast by the time I
got to the trailhead, which was along one of those famously
narrow English roads. I parked the car in the least obtrusive
place I could find, changed into some waterproof shoes, and
struck out. Within minutes, I wished I had Wellies, because I
was slogging through shin-deep mud and manure, thanks to
the wettest British winter in recent memory. Yet it was abso-
lutely worth it, because I was off the noisy motorway, traipsing
happily into the dusky silence of fields and woods, and was
once again acutely aware of God's presence. By the end of the
walk, a few hours later, the sun was gone and the stars hung
bright in the gloaming. Now and again I'd climb a dark hill,
emerge from copses of oak and silver birch, and stop to catch
my breath, reveling in a silence broken only by the occasional
bleating of distant sheep. Down in the budding glades glowed
the yellow lights of windows in distant cottages. The March air

was crisp and windless, and bore the faint but not unpleasant smell of wet earth and manure. I stood still for a while, utterly alone, an ocean away from my family, and yet I was anything but lonely under the light of the night's first stars. Somewhere in the darkness below me was my trusty rental car, and I knew it was time to go. I passed through a stile to the last field and surprised a flock of sheep. They bleated their irritation as I trudged down the hill, scattering them as I went. By the time I got back to my car, my shoes were heavy with mud and the legs of my pants were soaked.

I changed in the dark and drove to Stratford-upon-Avon for dinner at a pub called The Old Thatch, which has been there since 1470. Shakespeare was born a mere 300 yards away. Under oak beams older than America I ate shepherd's pie and read my George MacDonald book, grateful beyond words that the Lord had seen fit to give me the gift of a good day of solitude, that I had walked through old groves in the Forest of Arden, where the trees and brooks and stones speak to us of their maker, if we have ears to hear. Shakespeare wrote, "And this our life, exempt from public haunt, finds tongues in trees, books in the running brooks, sermons in stones, and good in everything. I would not change it."

Nor would I, Shakespeare. The Comforter found me there.

VII

THE ENCHANTED GROVE

Though nothing can bring back the hour
Of splendour in the grass, of glory in the flower;
We will grieve not, rather find
Strength in what remains behind;
In the primal sympathy
Which having been must ever be;
In the soothing thoughts that spring
Out of human suffering.
—William Wordsworth

As I've said, in the landscape of my childhood, I think of Illinois as the Garden and Florida as the Fall. Though there were important similarities—in the size of the towns, the church parsonages, the surrounding agrarian culture— the places could scarcely have been more different. I've often described it like this: I had been plucked out of a Norman Rockwell painting and plunged into the dark heart of a Flannery O'Connor story.

The trees were wildly different. In Florida there was a whole buzzing, humid forest of them, as compared to the broad farm- land of Monticello. In Illinois, folks had a Midwestern lack of accent, a way of talking that was to me as wide open and simple as the Great Plains; in Florida the accent was so thickly Southern I had a hard time understanding the other kids in school. I was often called a Yankee, and had to ask my parents what that meant. In Illinois I had the illusion (till just before we left) that I was a good little boy. In Florida my heart left the straight and narrow and mucked about in the swamplands. The change between those two cultures, those two geographies, those two galaxies, was jarring, and I've spent most of my adult life sorting out what it did to my young heart.

Let me give you an idea of what I'm talking about. When I was nine and we lived in Jacksonville, my brother and I went to the forbidden railroad tracks to goof around in the glade below the berm, and we stayed later than we were supposed to. My dad was upset because we had made him late for a church function, so rather than giving my brother and me a night at home with the Atari, he took us to the church and made us wait in his office for our punishment. It likely would have been nothing more than a stern talking to, but for some reason I can't now understand, I decided it would be better if we ran away. My older brother didn't want to, but somehow I talked him into it. We burst out of the office at sundown, ran the mile or so back home, rifled through my dad's desk drawer for change, and escaped with $2.64 in the pockets of our Wranglers. We planned to live behind the local Publix and make money by helping people load their groceries into their cars. But first, we had to survive the night in the woods behind the convenience store. My brother and I hid back there till well after dark, by which point my parents had notified the police. We were sure to be caught behind the store, so we shimmied through culverts and flattened ourselves in the weeds as police spotlights swept the roadsides. Around midnight we decided the jig was up and started the shameful walk home. One of the church elders drove by and spotted us crossing the street. "You boys need to get home," was all he said. When we walked through the front door, Mom and Dad fell to their knees and hugged us. They were crying. They had called the police, then the church, and then went from door to door in the neighborhood asking if anyone had seen two missing boys. The worst part was the way the kids at school the next day stared at me like I was a freak. I was a pariah from there on out, in their minds and in my own.

I got in a few fights. Corporal punishment was a thing back then, so I was regularly spanked by teachers and principals—and I regularly deserved it. I lied constantly about my whereabouts. Kids showed me terrible things that polluted my imagination. I could turn on the preacher's kid smile for the grown-ups, but I knew it concealed a wretched heart.

It wasn't just the world *within* me that was dark, though it was certainly dark enough for trouble. It was the world around me, too. It was sinister, more dangerous than I could have believed a year prior. The first summer we lived in Florida, when I was eight, there was a weedy cul-de-sac at one end of the unfinished neighborhood, where my brother and I sometimes shot bullfrogs with a BB gun so we could fry up the legs. One day I rode my bike down there and discovered a dead pig, at least as big as I was, cut open and crawling with maggots. I poked at it with a stick for a few minutes, repulsed and fascinated in equal measure, then ran home and told my dad about it. He investigated and said that it looked like it had been a part of an occult ceremony. Sadly, that wasn't the only time the occult turned up. Once, my cousin took me to an abandoned house deep in the woods to show me the pentagrams painted on the wall, the spent candles on the floor, and blood-red paint splashed everywhere. There were also murders in town. I vividly remember the day serial killer Ted Bundy was executed at the prison, just six miles from my house. There was racism (I remember a riot after a football game), and drug abuse, and violent fights at school, not to mention promiscuity (among the kids) and sexual abuse (also among the kids).

I need to reiterate that there were plenty of good things, too. But the culture shock that came with the move to Florida taught me this:

I was not the golden boy I thought I was.

The world was darker than I dreamed.

That's not to say I wouldn't have become starkly aware of these things had we stayed in Monticello; I most certainly would have, in one way or another. But the dividing line of childhood (Eden) and adolescence (Exile) seems, in the admittedly murky way we make sense of our own stories, easily placed between the two locations.

———

My parents were both native Floridians, Southern to the core, though they met in Georgia at what used to be called Atlanta Christian College. Their Southern accents probably lost some of the edge during their ten years in Illinois, so it didn't get handed down, but when they got back to Florida it returned with a vengeance, which left me in the curious position of thinking of myself as a non-Southerner surrounded, at home *and* at school, by a deep and disorienting Southernness.

plagued by their own guilt and shame. Go easy on them. Kids I thought were jerks based purely on the fact that they were jocks grew up to be elders and deacons at my dad's church. I bumped into them at Thanksgiving or Christmas services, and when they seemed so kind and interested in me and my family I realized that I had missed out on what might have been good friendships. I guess we all needed to grow up a little.

Second, I'd tell myself to pay attention to where I was. So many of the folks in school seemed resigned to life in Lake Butler, but I was having none of it. To go back to It's a Wonderful Life, I was George Bailey, dying to shake the dust of that crummy old town off my feet so I could see the world. There was a definite Tookishness in me, a longing to see mountains—*mountains*, Gandalf!—and vast cities and exotic cultures. The world was wider than Union County, Florida, and perhaps I knew it better than some others because I had come there from elsewhere—specifically the wild and exotic reaches of central Illinois. That wanderlust has been with me as long as I can remember. During our family's short stint in the Jacksonville suburbs, I often rode my bike to the railroad tracks that snaked along the St. John's River (the ones that got me into trouble before), walked farther along them than was prudent, and positively ached to keep going, just to see where I'd end up. Once I met a young man with a backpack, taking a break from his long journey and leaning against the railroad crossing sign. I was only about nine years old, but I ran home and packed a bag, fully intending to follow him. When I got back to the tracks, however, he was gone. I was stuck. So those years in Lake Butler were excruciating. We were confined to the smallest county in the state of Florida, and in my snobbish way I assumed I was among the smallest imaginations, too. Now, of course, I see how wrong I was. Consider this my formal apology to Lake Butler.

The problem wasn't Florida. The problem was me. All those live oaks and pines were full of wonder, but I refused to see it. I didn't know that the prison wasn't Lake Butler—it was myself. I loathed who I was, but I could neither articulate nor admit that, so I projected that loathing on anyone or anything around me. It may sound like I'm being too hard on myself. Maybe I am. There were plenty of good days, too. But they don't make my sin any less true.

Coming to Nashville ten years later with Jamie, as a Christian who was awestruck by how good the Good News was—that God knew him and yet loved him enough to put a ring on his finger, call him his beloved son, and throw a party—meant starting fresh. I was by no means perfect, but at the very least I knew I was forgiven, and those tiny seeds are still growing into sweeping branches where birds make their nests. We came here almost a quarter century ago, and it is a truer home than I've ever known. That's the good part. The bad part? Going back to where I grew up is hard. As soon as I cross the Florida State line, a dark mist gathers around my ankles and begins to work its way up to my heart. The memories sting. The accent sneaks back into vowels. Voices of regret fill my head. Questions churn up from the still waters and I begin to wonder, first, why I let my selfishness hurt people, and second, why I was so hurt—because *some* of the pain wasn't my fault. Some of it was passed on to me by other broken people. The mental picture I carry is of a little boy from Monticello, lost in the sylvan wilds of Florida, weeping under the live oaks because his innocence is gone and will never be recovered. He suspects that the root cause of his exile is some poisonous flaw that he carries with him wherever he goes, a sickness that has seeped down from the soles of his feet and into sandy earth of Florida, where it took shape as some scrounging beast that haunts the woods. If he can run fast enough, or hop the train, or disappear into a book, maybe he can find refuge, or at least forget for a little while that he's doomed.

Oh, how I love that kid. I wish I could tell him what I know now: there is a presence in the woods that is older and stronger and kinder than the ghost that harries him. If he would stand still enough to let it, that presence would overtake the poison, seep up through his feet and into his heart like a magic vine, and transform the dark forest into a garden of wonders.

When my oldest son turned twelve, his grandmother bought him a book called *The Yearling*. She said it was her favorite book as a girl. I had heard of it, of course. The Pulitzer Prize–winning author, Marjorie Kinnan Rawlings, lived just an hour south of Lake Butler, in a village near Micanopy called Cross Creek. She was our most famous local author. My parents had encouraged me to read *The Yearling* many times, but as a teenager I wasn't interested. It was about a kid with a deer, and the deer dies. What more do you need to know? I had seen *Old Yeller* and *Where the Red Fern Grows*. I had read *Sounder*. We all know how these stories go. Not only that, there was a distinct lack of dragons, dwarves, and elves. But the real strike against the book wasn't just the lack of fantasy accoutrements. It was that the book was set in Florida. Not just Florida—*my* part of Florida, the very place I wanted to escape more than any place in all the world. Why would I want to spend weeks on a book like that? It would be akin to escaping one jail cell only to get locked in another.

Thirty years passed.

The book found its way to The Warren, by way of a grandparent, bypassing a generation and coming into the hands of a little boy for whom Florida was not a pejorative word. Aedan finished it and told me, with tears in his eyes, that it was the best book he'd ever read. That gave me pause, because Aedan is a big reader, and I respected his taste even when he was twelve. With a few decades of distance between me and Lake Butler I decided that perhaps it was time to find out what all the fuss was about, so with some trepidation I opened the book, stepped through a flimsy screen door into the humid forests of childhood, and began.

From the opening scene, I was hooked. Twelve-year-old Jody Baxter is supposed to be doing his chores, but he sneaks away to a spring in the woods, where he hides in an alcove and makes a water wheel (a "flutter-mill") out of palmetto leaves. He lies there in the solitude, lost in the magic of the spinning wheel, and falls asleep. The way Rawlings described the sand pines, the tar-flower, the fetter-bush and sparkleberry, stirred in my heart a surprising affection for the land of my youth.

It seemed a strange thing to him, when earth was earth and rain was rain, that scrawny pines should grow in the scrub, while by every branch and lake and river there grew magnolias. Dogs were the same everywhere, and oxen and mules and horses. But trees were different in different places.

"Reckon it's because they can't move none," he decided. They took what food was in the soil under them.

The east bank of the road shelved suddenly. It dropped below him twenty feet to a spring. The bank was dense with magnolia and loblolly bay, sweet gum and gray-barked ash. He went down to the spring in the cool darkness of their shadows. A sharp pleasure came over him. This was a secret and a lovely place.[3]

3. Marjorie Kinnan Rawlings, The Yearling (1938; repr., New York: Scribner, 2001), 3.

A secret and a lovely place, like the Thinking Tree in Monticello. As I read, I felt the furniture of my memories rearranging as if by poltergeist. All at once the possibility arose that even in Florida there were secret and lovely places. The disdain I had felt for Lake Butler for so many years began to dissolve into the tiniest glimpse of wonder, which is enough to change a life. Only minutes prior, I wouldn't have believed the flora and fauna of North Florida worth much consideration, then suddenly I wanted to lie beside the bubbling spring with young Jody to watch the flutter-mill spin. More than that, I wanted to be young. Innocent. Able to be enchanted by the deep woods, astonished by magnolias. Somehow, along the way of adolescence, I had lost the ability to see—to really *see*—what glory God had lavished on that corner of the world to which I had been transplanted. Marjorie Rawlings hadn't grown up in Florida, but had lost her heart to it after her first visit from Washington, D.C. She moved south and loved it so much she never left. How had I so completely missed it?

The answer, it turned out, lay in the book. I just had to keep reading. I followed Jody's story, superimposing my own at nearly every turn, so much so that I wouldn't have been surprised to spot the little boy version of myself hiding behind one of those skinny pines near Jody's cabin.

At the risk of spoiling it for you, early in the book Jody finds an orphaned fawn, and his parents begrudgingly allow him to raise it. The pages of *The Yearling* are home to rattle-snakes, alligators, bears, and panthers, as well as a host of odd backwoods characters, but my favorite is Jody's father, Penny Baxter. Penny is a hardworking, rugged man trying to make a home for his family in the wild woods, and yet, tough as he is, he shows a tenderness to his little boy that Jody's mom, Ma Baxter, often doesn't. When she scolds Jody for slacking, Penny's gentler demeanor softens the blow, saying in effect, "Let the boy be a boy for a little while longer."

You may argue that I've given you the biggest spoiler of all by telling you at the outset that the deer dies. In this case, I happen to think that knowing adds to the sweet melancholy of the story, because without that tragic end gathering like a dark cloud on the horizon the narrative might read more like one of those meandering, nothing-really-happens stories of the mid-twentieth century that bore me silly. But as you follow the trail through the woods along with Jody, knowing what he does not about the fate of the deer, the dramatic irony serves to heighten the sense of foreboding and gives each lovely interaction between boy and fawn a fleeting tenderness it wouldn't otherwise have. Poor Jody doesn't yet know how hard life can be. In a sense, he's still in Monticello, where life's hammer blow hasn't yet fallen. Jody doesn't realize what we do: the snake is already loose in the garden.

I may have spoiled it by telling you *that* the deer dies, but it's all in the *how*. If you've ever longed for the innocence of youth again, if you've ever wished you could recover some of the wonder of the flutter-mill, if you've ever wept over the hurt you've given and the hurt you've received, then the final act's march into the gathering storm is the best and worst kind of medicine.

Aedan's grandmother told me, after she gave him the book, "I didn't realize when I was a little girl that the yearling

I was forty when I read *The Yearling*. My oldest son was twelve, the age at which I was lost in the Florida woods. I have tried to protect all three of my children, however falteringly, from the grief that hovers on the horizon of their lives like a gathering storm. But there's nothing for it. They're going to wound and get wounded. Seeing your children's innocence fray can remind you of the shredded grave cloth of your own, and memories long buried claw their way out of the earth to demand answers. *What happened to me? Why are these sins so persistent? Why am I so prone to wander these particular footpaths into destruction? Why*, I ask with Penny Baxter, *were my guts tore out—and why can't I keep the same from happening to my dear ones?* This is the bone-deep cry of humanity, from Job to Solomon to Marjorie Kinnan Rawlings, and even to Jesus himself: *Why, God?* We all know that we're as broken as the world, victims and villains all of us, with no hope but Christ for healing.

But even in Christ, the grief goes on, and anyone who tells you otherwise is in denial. That's not to say deep joy doesn't perpetually encroach, because like a waxing moon, the very fullness of joy is destined to one day wholly illuminate our faces. As C. S. Lewis says, in so many words, the sorrow now is part of the joy later. If the grief persists, you ask, then what good is the gospel? Because we do not grieve like those without hope. No, I can't stop the world from hurting my kids, any more than I can stop my kids from hurting the world in one way or another—but hope places the sorrow in a larger context, gives it a *telos*, assures the lost boy in the woods that he's not alone. I used to wish the boy could find his way out of the woods; now I want him to know that the woods have always been enchanted, and he was meant to make a home there for a while.

I read the last page, closed the book, and doubled over with tears, yearning to recover the little boy I used to be, and heartbroken that I couldn't. The wardrobe was locked. It was a Sunday afternoon, and I was on the front porch of The Warren. Aedan happened to look outside and see his old man sobbing, and in the most wonderful reversal of roles, he comforted me with a hug. The boy assured the man that whatever was wrong, it would be all right. In the weeks that followed I made my peace with Florida. Yes, it's still the strangest state in the Union by a long shot (the memes ain't wrong, y'all), but I could no longer deny that its tangle of trees holds a certain loveliness, an Edenic mystery of their own that *The Yearling* finally helped me to see. Rawlings wrote a tragedy about the death of childhood, yet to me it was a fairy tale that somehow resurrected mine.

I wrote a song called "The Ballad of Jody Baxter," an imagined conversation between me and a grown-up version of Jody. I recorded it on an album called *Light for the Lost Boy*—an album about the loss of innocence and the longing for the New Creation. To this day, it's one of my favorite lyrics to sing.

> *Do you remember, Jody Baxter, when the whippoorwill*
> > *sings*
> *How you stole across the pasture to the little hidden spring*
> *And you laid down by the water on a bed of Spanish moss*
> *And dreamed?*

When the wind was on the prairie and the fire was in the
    stove
With the wood you had to carry from the corner of the grove
But your daddy let you disappear with all your fishing gear
Into the cove?

It was good, good, good
But now it's gone, gone, gone
And there's a little boy who's lost out in the woods
Always looking for the fawn

I remember, Jody Baxter, when I hid out in the corn
How the clouds were moving faster with the coming of the
    storm
And I knew that I had broken something I could not repair
And I mourned

'Cause, the field was green as Eden, but then it withered
    into brown
In the middle of my grieving, well, they came and cut it
    down
And I was sure that it was all my fault
The day they mowed the garden to the ground

And what was good, good, good
Was gone, gone, gone
And there's a little boy who's lost out in the woods
Always looking for the fawn

So come back to me
Please, come back to me
Is there any way that we can change the ending
Of this tragedy?
Or does it have to be
This way?

I can see you, Jody Baxter, now you're broken by the years
As you lie down in the aster and you listen for the deer
And I'm a million miles away but I still pray the fawn can
    find me
Here

'Cause it was good, good, good,
But now it's gone
And I'm a little boy who's lost out in the woods
Always looking for the fawn

Later that year our family took the Micanopy exit off
Interstate 75, slowed the car to a crawl, and drove through
Marjorie Rawlings's sleepy old town, held in time by towering
boughs of live oaks. Spanish moss swayed in the breeze.
Sections of the shaded sidewalks had been slowly lifted into
disarray by the knotty oak roots, giving them the look of tombs
being pried open. We drifted on past the town to Cross Creek,
and to Marjorie's house, where she had sat on her screened-in
porch to type the story that transformed my grief to longing.
The Rawlings homeplace is now a state park and a National
Historic Landmark, and in fact it looks quite a bit like my
parents' place at Shiloh, with all manner of blossoming trees

and low-hanging fruit, sandy patches interspersed with grass, chickens pecking about in the groves.

We took the tour, and I sheepishly gave the tour guide my CD in case anyone wanted to hear the song the book had inspired. I doubt anyone ever did, and here's why. A display case in the hallway housed every edition of *The Yearling* from all over the world. Each cover featured an image of a little boy cradling a fawn, and the titles were written out in German, Norwegian, Japanese, Korean, Italian, Spanish—and the list went on. This story with which I had identified so closely was, it turns out, universal. If you ever want to be reminded that all humans are wounded and longing for healing, visit the Rawlings house. Look at all those book covers and believe a little easier that there was a Garden, then an Exile—but don't stop there, because the presence of the question is part of the answer. To quote old Jack Lewis again, if we find in ourselves a desire that nothing in this world can satisfy, maybe it's because we were made for another world.

Near the entrance to the homeplace there's a sign that bears Marjorie's own words, beckoning us deeper into the mystery of the trees:

> It is necessary to leave the impersonal highway, to step inside the rusty gate and close it behind. By this, an act of faith is committed, through which one accepts blindly the communion cup of beauty. One is now inside the grove, out of one world and in the mysterious heart of another. Enchantment lies in different things for each of us. For me, it is in this: to step out of the bright

sunlight into the shade of orange trees; to walk under the arched canopy of their jadelike leaves; to see the long aisles of lichened trunks stretch ahead in a geometric rhythm; to feel the mystery of a seclusion that yet has shafts of light striking through it. This is the essence of an ancient and secret magic. . . . And after long years of spiritual homelessness, of nostalgia, here is that mystic loveliness of childhood again. Here is home. An old thread, long tangled, comes straight again.[5]

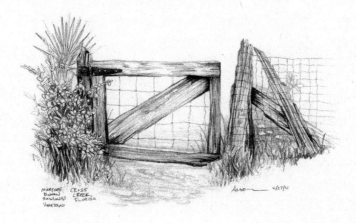

5. Inscription is from Rawlings's book *Cross Creek* (1942; repr., New York: Scribner, 1996), 15–16.

– VIII –

WE SHALL BE LED IN PEACE

And O, ye Fountains, Meadows, Hills, and Groves,
Forebode not any severing of our loves!
Yet in my heart of hearts I feel your might;
I only have relinquished one delight
To live beneath your more habitual sway.
I love the Brooks which down their channels fret,
Even more than when I tripped lightly as they;
The innocent brightness of a new-born Day
Is lovely yet.
—William Wordsworth

It might be too much to say that a garden saved my life, but at the very least a garden got me living again. If you've been paying attention, it should be evident that I'm an emotional guy. Most of the time that's good, especially if you're a song-writer. The practice of writing gets you out of your head and into your heart, then back into your head again. When you feel something deep and indecipherable, it's as if the waters of a subterranean lake have been disturbed. Songwriting is like putting on the scuba gear and diving down to find the source of the trouble. But the whole point is to drag it back to the surface so you can look at it, do a forensic test, and then publish an article. "Here's what I found, folks. Maybe it'll help you in your own deep dive." Not every song is like that, but the autobiographical ones are, for sure.

Back when my kids were hitting adolescence, some dormant dragon in the lake woke up and started thrashing around, churning up old bones to the surface. So I did the only thing I knew to do. I wrote about it. Those songs all ended up on *Light for the Lost Boy*, which was the record with the Jody Baxter song. The whole album, more or less, was about the loss of innocence—deep, subterranean waters, especially when you're turning forty. If the writing and recording process wasn't harrowing enough, I then went on tour to tell the stories for a few months. Every night the show opened with a video of several older people describing the Eden of their childhoods, then talking about the moments when they realized the world was broken and they were in exile. For some, it was their fathers leaving their mothers, and for some it was sexual abuse; for others it was the desecration of a beautiful landscape. After the video I'd sing a song called "Come Back Soon," which opens with the lines,

> *I remember the day of the Tennessee flood*
> *The sound of the scream and the sight of the blood*
> *My son, he saw as the animal died*
> *In the jaws of the dog as the river ran by*
> *I said, "Come back soon."*

> *It's there on the page of the book that I read*
> *The boy grew up and the yearling was dead*
> *He stood at the gate with the angel on guard*
> *And wept at the death of his little boy heart*
> *I said, "Come back soon."*

It was all downhill from there. I sang about Jody Baxter and the yearling. I sang about my son turning thirteen and growing into a world that I knew would wound him. There were songs about the inevitability of death, and my daughter's unanswerable questions, and the fields of Illinois corn being mowed to the ground. I sang about these things every single night. Without realizing it, I was on the verge of a breakdown. After years and years of hard touring, I was exhausted. My counselor asked if I'd ever had a sabbatical, and I laughed. Self-employed singer-songwriters don't get sabbaticals, I told him. On top of the exhaustion, there was this weird convergence of milestones and big changes. I turned forty; Jamie and I celebrated our twentieth wedding anniversary; I completed my record contract and had to decide whether to renew it; The Wingfeather Saga, which took a decade to write, was complete. There was more, but you get the idea. And in the middle of all that, I was singing every night about the loss of childhood and the yearning for resurrection. It was a perfect storm for a midlife crisis.

Some people buy Corvettes. I tumbled into a depression that lasted a couple of years. So many milestones converged in such a small space of time that it's no wonder I had emotional whiplash. But without the benefit of hindsight, I had no idea what was happening to me. It wasn't just one leviathan roiling the dark lake, it was a brood of them. All I knew was that I couldn't stop crying, and all my kids knew was that something was wrong with the papa.

The whole thing came to a head at a church in North Carolina, on the Behold the Lamb of God tour. That tour has been a complicated one over the years. On one hand, it's undeniably one of the great surprise blessings of my life. To this day I've never heard of a tour quite like it—one about the story of the Bible, told during the Christmas season, with a band of old friends who have come together each winter for twenty straight years. I shouldn't complain, obviously. It took a few years to realize that I experienced some kind of spiritual attack every time we took those songs on the road. Whether it was because I'm the point man on the tour or because I'm hyper-emotional, each time December approached I felt a mounting dread mixed in with all the joy and gratitude.

For some reason, being surrounded by all those wonderful and wonderfully-talented friends exacerbated some deep, festering wounds, so that after the two-hour concert and an hour of meet-and-greets each night, I'd get on the bus with a host of awful voices clamoring in my head. Everyone seemed to be fine but me, so I'd turn on Happy Andrew and suppress all the painful stuff. Truth be told, that works—for a while. At some point on every tour I'd end up in my bunk, or a stairwell backstage, or out on a walk behind the church after the show, seething with self-hatred and often crying. Again, I had no idea what was wrong. I just knew that I was hurting, and something about the tour was causing me pain—pain that was magnified somehow by the giddy joy of everyone else. .

That afternoon in North Carolina was a rough one. I had called Jamie to ask for prayer as I walked the empty halls of the big church building toward the stage for sound check. I could hear the echo of the band on stage, all of them goofing around and waiting for me to show up. Every step was more difficult than the last. As I turned to walk through a corridor to the stage, my head screaming with accusing voices, I spotted the open door of a janitor's closet. Without thinking, I ducked inside and stood in the dark behind the open door. My head was down. I remember praying, "God, please. Please send me some light. It feels so dark, and I just need some light."

Right after that prayer, someone from the church happened to walk by, and they closed the door. It felt like God was playing a cruel joke. I literally tumbled to the floor and began to sob. Outside the door the band sound-checked without me, and the sound of the music and laughter only served to widen my loneliness. I just couldn't stop crying. It felt like:

> my heart was being torn open
> whoever was doing the tearing
> wouldn't leave well enough alone
> they kept poking at the wounds
> worst of all, I had the sense that,
> though the voices in my head
> were from the pit of hell,
> the actual wounding
> was from the King of heaven
> it was as if I had been begging God
> to lift me out of the mud
> and I saw his hand reach down
> and merely push me deeper

It was one of the lowest, most desolate places I've ever been. I was in a tomb, and God wouldn't roll away the stone.

After about three hours of lying with my cheek on the floor, I looked at my phone and saw that I'd missed fifteen calls, from Jamie and friends in the band. I called Jamie back. My voice was a disembodied croak, frightening for both her and me to hear.

I told her where I was, she passed the word along, and two worried friends soon came to the closet to pray for me and help me to my feet. That's when I saw the literal puddle of tears on the floor, about eight inches around, next to the print of my face, and realized how terribly thirsty I was. Showtime was in five minutes, so just outside the door was a throng of people pouring into the church to find their seats. The guys told me to keep my head down because I looked like I'd been in a fist fight, then they walked me to the bus to make myself presentable. I felt stupid, and ugly, and ashamed. I changed clothes, splashed some water on my face, and did the show without a hitch. That was the most frightening part of all: that I could suppress that much internal chaos in a matter of minutes and put on a show without the audience knowing a thing was wrong.

Then came the awful shame of living the next two weeks in close quarters with a bus full of concerned friends. I didn't know how to explain to myself what was happening, so it was impossible to explain it to them. What I saw reflected in their loving eyes was a freak who couldn't get it together. It triggered a painful memory of a year at junior high church camp, when I got sick and had a fever dream in the tent with two of my friends. For some reason I woke up screaming and flailing, hitting them over and over. The worried dean shone his flashlight into the tent and I remember staring at the light and saying, "I'm sorry," over and over like he was God and I was facing the final judgment. (This happened at a camp site canopied, of course, by trees.) The next morning the kids all stared at me warily and I knew I was a pariah again, just like when my brother and I ran away. So I muscled through the tour with that as the chief thought in my head, singing every night about something I truly believed: that Jesus was God. But I was too scared to look at him, because the worst thing of all would be to see the freak in the reflection of his eyes, too.

Sometime after the tour those same friends who helped me out of the cave made an appointment with a local Christian counselor, and one of them even drove me down there to make sure I would go. If any of this sounds familiar and you've never considered talking to a saint with a degree in counseling, consider this a public service announcement. It did me a world of good, and from the very first meeting he began to dismantle narratives I had constructed to make sense of my pain. I'm a professional storyteller, so the stories I had been telling myself were elaborate and airtight. I could defend them all day long. It was only when I sat down with a counselor that I discovered how false they were. As I wrote in my last book, one of the first things he told me was this: "I've never met anyone who could correctly interpret their own childhood."

The more I told him the more I realized I wasn't a freak, I wasn't crazy, and so much of the shame I felt simply wasn't justified. I was a sinner, yes, but I had blamed myself for things that actually weren't my fault at all. The gospel broke through because it isn't just about the fact that we're all fallen—that part's easy for me to swallow—it's about the fact that we're perfectly loved. And that's the part I have a hard time believing on a minute-by-minute basis. Being around all those friends I admired so much just accentuated the feeling that I was a charlatan, and I believed it with all my heart, in spite of their kind words, in spite of their long-suffering companionship, in spite of the fact that every night I sang with all my strength of the mighty deeds of the Lord. "Jesus is God, and he loves you." That's the thesis statement of every concert I've ever played. I believe it completely. It's easier, though, to fling that glorious truth out to the masses than it is to let it settle deep into my own murky waters where the dragons writhe.

As it happened, early that year I was expected to make a new album. The studio was booked, but I honestly couldn't imagine doing it. After *Light for the Lost Boy*, after all the grief over the life changes, after the darkness of the janitor's closet, it felt ridiculous to enter the studio to write a bunch of songs. I joked with my producer, Gabe, that it was sure to be the most depressing album I'd ever made (which was saying something).

Looking back, it was the kindness of God that the two months set aside to make *The Burning Edge of Dawn* were March and April. I went into that record under the heavy, gray dreariness of Nashville's late winter. When I looked out the window at home all I saw was rain, rain, rain. When I looked inside at the weather of my soul all I saw was rain, rain, rain. Not only that, Gabe's studio on Music Row was in a windowless basement, which meant that when I wasn't looking out at the rain, I was in yet another cave.

Who knows the mind of our God? Did he conspire with time and the earth's ponderous tilt into the sunlight of spring so that every day his frail, beloved child would see the bashful opening of cherry blossoms and daffodils on the way to the studio? Did he know that whatever wound was in me would heal enough that I could begin to hope that the pain would subside? Did he know that I needed the cave to write about the light outside it?

One afternoon at The Warren, during a short break in the near-perpetual rain, I took my guitar out to a porch swing that hangs from a drooping hackberry limb. I was bundled in a coat, a scarf, and fingerless gloves. The guitar happened to be tuned to DADGAD, and I strummed a 6/8 pattern for a few minutes. The words that came were these:

> I tried to be brave, but I hid in the dark
> And I sat in that cave and I prayed for a spark
> To light up all the pain that remained in my heart
> And the rain kept falling

> Down on the roof of the church where I cried
> I could hear all the laughter and love and I tried
> To get up and get out, but a part of me died
> And the rain kept falling down

> I'm scared if I open myself to be known
> I'll be seen and despised and be left all alone
> So I'm stuck in this tomb and you won't move the stone
> And the rain keeps falling

Somewhere the sun is a light in the sky
But I'm dying in North Carolina and I
Can't believe there's an end to this season of night
And the rain keeps falling down

There's a woman at home and she's praying for light
My children are there and they love me in spite
Of the shadow I know that they see in my eyes
And the rain keeps falling

I'm so tired of this game, of these songs, of the road
I'm already ashamed of the line I just wrote
But it's true and it feels like I can't sing a note
And the rain keeps falling down

That was as much of the song as I could write. My fingers were cold, it started to rain again, and I felt a little embarrassed at the thought of sharing thoughts so raw with people I didn't know.

What happened next gets a little fuzzy. I can't remember which came first: Luci Shaw's poetry or the day I went out into our muddy back garden to plant seeds for spring. Soon after I started the song and gave up on it, though, Skye and I went outside with a little packet of seeds and a trowel. We knelt in the mud as I explained to her what we were doing. Just like Mr. Joey's-dad, I hefted the trowel in my hand, then stabbed it into the earth. I did it again, then again. I tore a furrow into the ground about a foot long, then laid the trowel aside and parted the dirt with my fingers.

THE WARREN IN WINTER
12/27/20

"What do you do now, Papa?" Skye asked.

"Now," I said with a smile, "we plant the seed." I gingerly took the little thing from the packet, pressed it into the mud, and covered it over. It was like a funeral. It was like that day in the janitor's closet when I asked God for help and instead of lifting me out he pushed me deeper. "This is how seeds grow."

And the rain fell, and the rain kept falling.

Luci Shaw's perfect little poem, called "Forecast," goes like this:

Planting seeds
Inevitably
Changes my feelings
About rain

There's a lot of truth and beauty in those eight little words. Kind of like seeds. Thanks to Luci, I knew how to finish the song.

My daughter and I put the seeds in the dirt
And every day now we've been watching the earth
For a sign that this death will give way to a birth
And the rain keeps falling

Down on the soil where the sorrow is laid
And the secret of life is igniting the grave
And I'm dying to live, but I'm learning to wait
And the rain keeps falling down

Can you believe that he loves you? Could it be that when you're deep in the dark cave, it's not because he doesn't love you, but because he does? I wasn't angry at the earth when I wounded it. Nor was I killing the seed when I buried it. I was giving it a chance to be born again.

———

Not long after that, my friend Julie gave our family the gift of a thirty-year garden plan. She knew I loved English gardens, so she crafted a blueprint for me to follow until I'm an old man. It's taken years—hours and hours of work digging the footpaths and packing them with sand before covering it all with pea gravel, building the rock walls to enclose the front garden, constructing the arch, weeding the accursed Bermuda grass (which I sometimes think is all I'll be doing for the next thirty years). Thanks to COVID, I was home this spring to work and keep the garden every day, and I'm happy to report that it's not too shabby. I've planted peonies, hollyhocks, Mexican feather grass, alchemilla mollis, Russian sage, fountains of catmint, tulips, Shasta daisies, hardy geraniums, clematis, echinacea, zinnias, daffodils, crocuses, yarrow, salvia, and lamb's ear. Now that the perennials are a few years old, they've filled in the gaps so that in early summer when I walk through the garden to the Chapter House it's among a chorus of honeybees and chirping finches. Late summer has brought the ruby-throated hummingbirds and a flurry of butterflies: gulf fritillaries, monarchs, red admirals, zebra swallowtails, tiger swallowtails, buckeyes, and hackberry emperors.

In a literal sense, God turned my grief into a garden. Joey's dad told me that the pansies under the live oak represented the kind things his daughter had done, and for me each seedling that sprouted was its own kindness, its own obedience to Christ's command to come forth from the grave.

I'm no master gardener, not by a long shot, but it's hard to imagine life without it now. In the early spring I can almost hear the garden calling me outside to pull weeds or deadhead flowers, to gasp at some new bloom that's opened up in quiet glory. After being indoors for hours at a time working on a story or a song, the sun on my face and the nearness of growing things rejuvenates me like nothing else.

A teaspoon of garden soil contains hundreds of millions of microbes, which means that gardeners tend to have a wider variety of gut bacteria. One of those is called *mycobacterium vaccae* which, when it gets under your fingernails, releases serotonin in your system. Serotonin is a natural anti-depressant that also happens to strengthen our immune systems.[6] According to Sue Stuart-Smith, in her book *The Well-Gardened Mind*, our bodies experience healing merely being *near* the color green, and "nature's restorative effects on the cardiovascular system are demonstrable in the body within a few minutes."[7] It's crazy, but it's almost like God knew what he was doing when he made humans to be gardeners in the first place.

Gardening is, fundamentally, an act of hope. When I put bluebell bulbs in Warren Wood in the fall, I'm also planting hope that I'll be around in the spring to watch their little green spikes splay out of the brown earth down by the creek. Every morning in the spring I bundle up and go on what my neighbor calls a "beauty hunt." I don't come in until I find at least one sign of new life. And it's always, always there.

And now, when the sky is heavy and gray and the rain keeps falling? I rejoice. I've planted seeds, you see, and my feelings about rain have changed. Something good is coming.

Every spring, it's inevitable.

---

6. Sue Stuart-Smith, *The Well-Gardened Mind: Rediscovering Nature in the Modern World* (New York: Scribner, 2020), 79.
7. Stuart-Smith, *The Well-Gardened Mind*, 74.

IX

FOOTPATHS

Then sing, ye Birds, sing, sing a joyous song!
And let the young Lambs bound
As to the tabor's sound!
We in thought will join your throng,
Ye that pipe and ye that play,
Ye that through your hearts to-day
Feel the gladness of the May!
—William Wordsworth

In the gladness of May 2020, thanks to a traffic jam and the Waze app on my phone, I discovered my favorite road in the county on the way home from Chipotle. To help you avoid congestion, the app sometimes sends you home in surprising ways, so after more than two decades in Nashville I discovered a back way to The Warren via Old Smyrna Rd. Because the road is old, the road is narrow. Because it's narrow, there are speed humps every fifty yards. Because of the speed humps, you drive slow enough to take in the drystone walls, the ancient trees, the historical marker signs, the views of farmsteads nearly as old as the Revolutionary War. In Hugh Walker's 1970 book *Tennessee Tales*, I happened upon this entry about Old Smyrna Road:

> In a narrow valley on [the] farm a beech forest once stood, through which, it is believed, a buffalo trail had passed . . . and just a few miles away was the site of an ancient Indian village. . . . One giant beech tree is

still standing . . . and a state forester said it could be over four hundred years old. The beech tree had many names and dates. . . . But one name, near the ground, was so old and grown with the years it could not be read. It appeared to be a French name, with the prefix "la" or "de." But the date, in old-fashioned numbers, was plain—1563.[8]

It was thrilling to discover that road and the entry in that book within a span of a few weeks. If there were beech trees that old in Brentwood, maybe Cane Ridge had some Treebeards deep in the woods, too. The Cane Ridge Community Club, a delightful gathering of locals old and young, meets once a month in what used to be a one-room schoolhouse on Cane Ridge Road. We've fallen out of the habit, but when we first moved here we went every month, partly out of a desire to be connected to the community and partly because the meetings featured a potluck dinner that tasted like my childhood in Lake Butler (99 percent of the deviled eggs I've ever eaten were at potluck dinners). I had met the president, Twana, a few years back because she and a local researcher were surveying all the family cemeteries in the area in order to preserve the history—and to keep them from being inadvertently bulldozed by developers. There's a nineteenth-century family cemetery in the woods just a short walk from The Warren, covered in leaves and easy to miss, so she pulled up our gravel drive in her truck one day to ask about it.

---

8. Hugh Walker, *Tennessee Tales* (Nashville, TN: Aurora Publishers, 1970).

After I read about the old beech with the 1563 date on it, I figured she was the perfect person to email about trees, and I wasn't wrong. She replied, "Yes, I found some huge ones when I was out hunting for cemeteries. Happy to show you." A few weeks later, Twana gathered a few other tree lovers in the community and we set out.

The first one she took us to was a gloriously knotty white oak with a seventeen-foot circumference towering in the woods near the interstate. I had blown past it on the interstate a thousand times and never knew. A short walk beyond the tree was a cemetery from the early 1800s with daffodils rising out of the humus around the graves. We drove to another giant oak (this one was nineteen feet around) that stood just inches from the edge of another development, having narrowly escaped being killed along with everything else. The only reason she knew these trees existed was because she had walked on her own two feet through the forest.

Which leads me to footpaths.

If we're hanging out for more than thirty minutes, chances are you'll hear me talk about them. I wish you could see my family wearily bow their heads when it comes up, bracing themselves for thirty minutes of wistful extolment of the virtues of English footpaths. When I say "footpaths," I don't mean sidewalks or greenways or hiking trails like we have here. I mean honest-to-goodness public footpaths that usher you off the impersonal highway and into the in-between places of fat, old trees and ancient ruins and babbling brooks, footpaths that cross fields of private property where sheep and cows graze, footpaths that get you from one town to the next without the danger of walking along the weedy shoulder of a busy road. I had no idea how marvelous a thing a footpath could be until my first visit to the English countryside.

THE DARK HEDGES
NORTHERN IRELAND   Andrew
                                                    12-26-20

Many Americans, I'm sure, get a taste of the English countryside and come home with the impression that the land is simply prettier there.[9] That's all there is to it, we think. They win. The rolling hills, the quiet rivers, the lushness of the forests, the idyllic pastures, the formal gardens—it seems

---

9. To be fair, it's not like England doesn't have litter, or its share of land misuse, or it's less-than-picturesque places. There's barbed wire and industrial blight there, too, and a lot of the lovely footpaths and villages like I've described are in places where the upper crust have much easier access—and not everybody in England has the time, the money, or the space for a verdant cottage garden. Some, I'm sure, will say that I'm painting too rosy a picture. To that I'd reply; "Go easy on me. I'm a romantic."

the beauty is just turned up a notch or two compared to what we have in the States. There's some truth to it. England's gentler, rainier climate does give it a horticultural advantage. In addition to the general wetness of the place, there's the rich gardening history. The flower garden of the 1700s was typically a formal affair only the elite could afford, but the love of growing more than just vegetables began to catch on in the lower classes thanks to the increasing availability (and affordability) of imported seeds from almost every continent.[10] The craze soon made Britain the gardening capital of the world, and it's arguably still true today.

I tend to be a little sheepish when I talk about my love of gardening, but over there it's fair to say that many Brits take gardening—whether cottage gardens, formal gardens, or vegetable gardens—more seriously than we Americans do. They don't call it the yard, but "the front garden" and "the back garden." They also have allotments, or in our parlance, "community gardens," for people without land, a tradition there that goes back hundreds of years. The idea that every house should have a square of pristine, unimaginative, freshly mowed grass out front is a mostly American thing. Over there, the smallest lawns aren't typically lawns at all, but rather are fenced in and landscaped, with winding walkways bordered by flowers up to the front door, where there's often an arrangement of

10. In the 1700s an American named John Bartram shipped plants and seeds from the New World to a Londoner named Peter Collinson. A Swede named Charles Linnaeus got involved, and next thing you know Britain was a gardening mecca. If you want to dig into the history, I commend to you Andrea Wulf's *The Brother Gardeners: A Generation of Gentlemen Naturalists and the Birth of an Obsession*.

potted plants. The windows are adorned with window boxes, and the walls and gables are covered in climbing rose vines. Admittedly, it's not unusual to see some nice arrangements in suburban American entryways, but they're always dwarfed by that grassy postage stamp of unused space we spend untold amounts of gasoline and sweat to keep up, called "the lawn." What's it for, anyway? Nobody's playing croquet out there.

It may sound like I'm bemoaning America, but I promise I'm not. (Not really.) Because after I came back from England for the second time and the initial thrill wore off, I began to notice something remarkable: what we have in Tennessee is *just* as beautiful as some of what I've seen in Britain and Ireland—just as green, just as effusive with wildlife (if not more so) and domesticated animals, hills that are just as shapely. I was reminded of it afresh when Twana led me across all that rolling farmland to find the trees that day. The road that winds through the countryside to The Warren and the nearby cluster of subdivisions is truly one of the best parts of living here: one minute you're hardly moving on a busy four-lane road, and the next you're in a car commercial, steering your way through a sun-dappled tunnel of trees, under a canopy of pin oaks and hackberries along a gracefully twisting road.

We drive that road so often that our kids named the highlights—Asher did, anyway, because he's the quietly funny one. At the crest of a hill above the road there's a barbed wire fence, beyond which several cows usually graze. Aedan often gazed wistfully out the window and said, "I love that hill," so Asher dubbed it "Dan's Crest." Now the boys are grown men, but if we happen to be in the car together when we pass it, it's not unusual to hear Asher's now-deeper voice mutter, "There's Dan's Crest." After Dan's Crest, the road dips into a picturesque little valley where a herd of Black Angus cows hang out. There's a muddy cattle pond where you'll often spot great herons standing still as statues. Beyond the pond and all along the slope of the surrounding hill, the livestock graze in a wide bowl of bright green grass. Asher named that part of the drive, "The Valley of Mordu," because, you know, "more doo."

One day I realized that the Valley of Mordu was as beautiful as the most beautiful bits of England that I love, but for some reason I didn't get the same flutter in the stomach I feel over there. It wasn't just the familiarity. Something was different but it took me a while to put my finger on it. If it's just as pretty, why isn't the Tennessee countryside as vaunted and cherished as the English one? Class, can you name the difference? Anyone? Okay, fine. I'll give you the answer:

FOOTPATHS.[11]

Without public footpaths, there's no way for me to walk through that pasture without trespassing. I'll never know, short of an awkward conversation with the landowner, what lies beyond Dan's Crest, or what it's like to stroll among the grazing cattle of the Valley of Mordu. In England, you see, they have public footpaths—140,000 miles of them, in fact—which are rights of way for walkers. And I don't just mean sidewalks. I

---

11. To be fair, there are quite a few possible answers here. But for my purposes they represent a mindset that the land is a civic good, a shared responsibility, and not something to be merely divvied up and monetized. There may not be public footpaths in much of Europe, but the beauty of the landscape there is due in part to centuries of cultivation and care for the land as a common blessing.

mean trails that lead away from the sidewalk, over stone walls, and straight across fields of wheat. If the landowner is out there on his tractor, he won't call the cops; he'll just give you a polite nod and wish you well on your way to Rivendell. If there are cows, it's on you to avoid being trampled by them. Fingerposts are scattered along the roadsides, beckoning travelers to park the car and see the countryside from within. It's hardly an exaggeration to call it miraculous. At least that's how this American sees it. Friends in the U.K. seem surprised by my passion for footpaths, because it's a way of life for them. But it might not have been. The right to ramble across the land didn't happen by accident, and there was a long and hard-fought battle for nearly a century to make it legal again after the upper-class landowners of the late nineteenth century slowly cut off the general public from enjoying the beauty of the island. For many years, it didn't look like the ramblers would win. But they did, and I'm so glad.[12]

---

12. Mike Parker's *The Wild Rover* offers a succinct history of the whole thing, tracing the various demonstrations and bills that were lobbied to secure the enjoyment of Britain's vast beauty for the common folk. Even though the footpaths had been used by the public for centuries to get around, wealthy landowners got territorial and hired guards to keep people off their land, ostensibly to protect the grouse (or whatever) they wanted to hunt. The Industrial Revolution meant that thousands of people spent their days laboring miserably in smog-ridden cities like Manchester and they understandably felt they had a right to enjoy their weekends walking in the fresh air of the nearby moors and mountains. The fight took decades, with small victories here and there, but by and large the calls for public access to the natural beauties of Britain were ignored by the government. After World War II, though, England was in a bad way and the people were desperate for some good news, which at last led to the government's creation of the Pennine Way, along with several other long walks and the designation of Areas of Outstanding

One of the great joys of my life has been the hours upon hours that my family and I have wandered through the hills of England on footpaths, over drystone walls by way of stiles, through kissing-gates, and even along private driveways to a gate in someone's back garden that leads right through a meadow of grazing sheep. Growing up surrounded by farmland from which I was forever cut off, it's difficult to articulate how intensely delightful it feels to hobbit my way across a meadow of golden grain, with a map in one hand and a walking stick in the other. In America I'm only ever allowed to see the Valley of Mordu from the road—in glances if I'm driving, or for a few seconds if I'm not. I've lived here for twenty-three years and I've never strolled through the prettiest valley in our vicinity. I'm sure that, in the deep woods beyond Mordu, clear springs bubble up from the limestone, creeks babble through gullies; I'm sure there are ruins visible as mossy foundation stones and monolith chimneys covered in vines, not to mention old graves and Civil War trenches and the remains of Native American settlement—but I'll never, ever know it because it's on private property and I'd be either arrested or staring down the barrel of a landowner's Smith & Wesson, blubbering "I'm friends with Twana, I swear."

In the same way that I believe Mill Creek would have fewer dishwashers dumped into it if only people could really see it, and therefore cherish it, the land around us would be better protected, better loved, if we were able to enjoy it on foot.

Natural Beauty. Soon those in charge of the Ordnance Survey maps acquiesced and displayed the public footpaths, and now guys like me can wander the Shire for days without fear of Farmer Maggot's wrath.

I happen to think that Nashville's countryside would be as legendary as England's. But without experiencing how good a right to roam could be, it's a tough sell. Certain bad actors would abuse it, for a while, at least. It would take a few years for our culture to learn how wonderful it would be to trust and be trusted. But before that happened people would get mad. Someone would get attacked by cows (this actually happens in England) and the farmer would get sued (this actually *doesn't* happen in England) and the fun would be over.

Footpaths were once how people got around in England, and though they're mostly recreational nowadays, they're still a reliable way to get from one town to the next. We have just as many rivers, creeks, and waterfalls, just as many beautiful vistas, but our individualism has cut us off from one of the best things about this continent: the land—unless we drive two hours to a state park.

Did you know that there's such a thing as a pub walk? (I should point out before going any further that pubs in the U.K. aren't anything like the bars we have here. In the U.S., bars are dark and noisy, sometimes seedy joints with flatscreens everywhere and the music turned up so loud you have to shout. Village pubs, on the other hand, are community establishments, places to sit in a snug and visit with your friends— more like a coffeehouse that's been there for five hundred years. Children and dogs are welcome. Families go there for dinner.) You can buy a book of suggested pub walks, complete with a description of the history of the pub (e.g., "Shakespeare and C. S. Lewis frequented this establishment—not at the same time, obviously," or "this was Rupert Brooke's favorite chair in which to chortle" or "this has been a pub since 1146, so there"), suggestions for their signature meals, and finally a map to a circular walk on footpaths that explore a few miles of the surrounding countryside. The idea is that you park at the pub, go on a woody ramble, then reward yourself with a plate of fish and chips or sticky toffee pudding at the end. Now imagine the nearest equivalent in the U.S.: a Waffle House walk! You park at the yellow bastion of yumminess, dodge traffic, try not to trip over broken sidewalks (if there are any) while taking in views of loading docks behind Kroger and the lovely disarray of power lines overhead, before you return five minutes later, as scattered and smothered as the hashbrowns. Before you object, remember this: the land where all that stuff is built is *just as pretty as Britain's*. It's just been asphalted over or blocked by chain-link fences with NO TRESPASSING signs.

My frustration isn't with America's geography. This place is so beautiful I can hardly believe it sometimes. It's maddening, though, to love it this much and to feel like we're only peeking out at it through the blinds, unable to really experience the beauty that stretches out for miles beyond the window. In *The Wild Rover*, Mike Parker tells of how he set out to walk every footpath within three miles of his home in Wales: "My footpath audit had been a revelation. Within three miles of my front door, I walked nearly 70 miles of rights of way, from gloomy squelches through dank forestry to hawthorn-trimmed holloways high over the hills. I found lakes, woods, views, and neighbors that I never knew existed."[13] *Seventy miles* of footpaths

---

13. Mike Parker, *The Wild Rover: A Blistering Journey Along Britain's Footpaths* (London: HarperCollins, 2011), 16.

in a three-mile radius. I drive 2.8 miles to our nearest Kroger. Imagine all the little wonders that could be discovered between here and there if only I were allowed to roam this lovely Tennessee countryside. Imagine the encounters with other walkers, the wildlife, the cemeteries, the ruins, the sightings of old trees towering in the glades.

———

I couldn't stop thinking about that great old beech tree with the date carved into it, so I drove the fifteen minutes over to Old Smyrna Road, determined to find it if it was still there at all. Sneed Acres, the first historic home I stopped at, had an official marker out front telling of its establishment as a plantation in 1798. There were cars in the driveway beyond the open iron gate, but after I got out of the car I saw the NO TRESPASSING sign. I stood there trying to decide whether or not to approach the house, saw a black skull-and-crossbones flag out back (no joke), and eagerly got back in my car. I drove to another historical marker, this one in front of an old brick building in the colonial style. It wasn't renovated, so I felt less likely to be reported to the police. The marker said that the house was built on the site of a Native American town, and in the early 1800s it took the name Cottonport. The town, if it could have been called that, included a grist mill, a cotton gin, a general store, and a post office. Now it was a rather plain house in an area surrounded by uppity new construction. I happened to see a young man getting out of his car in the driveway and I awkwardly asked if he knew anything about an old beech tree with writing on it.

"No, but my granddaddy might. He grew up here and he lives next door."

He walked me over and introduced me to his grandfather, a matter-of-fact old man with a wonderful drawl. The man told me that his great-great-great-great grandfather was the one who had founded Cottonport. He also had a lot to say about all the new neighbors who had razed the woods and built fancy houses without a care for the history of the place. I asked if he had found any Native American artifacts, and he said, "Of course," as if it was a dumb question. I guess it was. "The folks who bought the back of the property built a barn right on top of an Indian burial ground. They tried to get 'em to stop, but they didn't care. They found a family cemetery out in the middle of their horse pasture, and folks come and fenced it up to protect it. But as soon as the authorities left, they tore down the fence and let their horses walk all over it again. These folks don't care about nothing." He looked out the window. "I tell you, the worst thing is that I've lived long enough to see it turn into this."

"Do you know anything about an old beech tree?" He shook his head. "The book here says it had writing on it dating back to the 1500s. Does that ring a bell?"

"Oh, I do remember that tree," he said. "It's gone now. They cut it down when they built a subdivision over there."

We let our shared grief fill the silence for a few moments, then I asked, "Are there any other old trees that you remember from growing up here?"

"Well, there's that old catawba tree out front." Its trunk was huge and gloriously twisted. Many of the lower branches were dead but there were large leaves greening the top.

"Do you happen to know how old it is?"

"Naw, but it's looked just like that since I was a little boy."

I kept hoping he'd offer to let me poke around in his woods, but no such luck. I thanked him and moved on, consulting the map on my phone to see if there were any access points to the woods. I drove a few miles around to the entrance of the subdivision he mentioned, got out of my car, and followed a walking path along the creek—the same creek that likely would have bubbled up from Cottonport's spring, which was the water source that attracted the Native Americans to it centuries ago. It was beautiful, really, even with all the subdivision houses flanking the walkway. I saw tall sugar maples that had to be 200 years old, towering sycamores (again, with their "sudden whiteness"), and green ashes heavy with vines. The walkway ended in a wall of tall goldenrod and purple ironweed into which the creek disappeared upstream. Monarchs and zebra swallowtails danced in the air above the flowers. I pushed a few feet into the brush to see how hard it would be, still hoping the old man was mistaken and I would spot that five-hundred-year-old beech, but it was no use. The weeds were too thick, and I was getting devoured by mosquitoes. Too bad. I sure hope that somewhere in those woods, there's a monumental beech that sprouted at the end of the Middle Ages, but I'll never know. Why? Glad you asked. Because there aren't any footpaths.

On the walk back along the creek to my car, I was struck by the fact that after thirty minutes of walking along a babbling brook, among tall wildflowers and late-summer butterflies, I didn't encounter a single person. Sure, there were folks pushing baby strollers up on the subdivision road, but no one down in the valley where the real beauty was.

———

A few years back, the C. S. Lewis foundation invited me to Cambridge for a concert and a lecture, so I had exactly three days to see what there was to see. I asked a few locals to recommend the best walk, and the consensus was Grantchester Meadows. I bought a map and struck out, first along King's Parade, a breathtaking avenue that affords the best view of the ancient college, including the centerpiece, King's College Chapel. The Chapel is breathtaking with its buttery stone, Gothic spires, and massive stained-glass window gazing out over the busy street. I attended church there one morning for a service presided over by the poet Malcolm Guite, and lost myself in the architectural intricacy of the ceiling, just as Wordsworth described in his sonnet, "Inside of King's College Chapel, Cambridge."

> These lofty pillars, spread that branching roof
> Self-poised, and scooped into ten thousand cells,
> Where light and shade repose, where music dwells
> Lingering—and wandering on as loth to die;
> Like thoughts whose very sweetness yieldeth proof
> That they were born for immortality.

After the chapel I followed a narrow alley to the parkland behind the colleges, called "The Backs." I crossed a bridge and walked along the River Cam, with its long, lazy punts gliding tourists beside the ancient college buildings. Out past the school and across broad green parks I walked, to the plainer district of the city. After a long stretch of rather uninteresting row houses, always consulting my map to be sure I hadn't taken a wrong turn, I eventually ended up at what looked like a dead end: a gravel parking lot bordered by hedges. I was disappointed until I spotted a gate at one end, beside which stood one of those wonderful wooden public footpath signs, beckoning me into another world.

I passed through the gate and was greeted at once by about thirty inconsiderate cows blocking the path, all of them lying in the muck and chewing the cud. Apologizing under my breath, I threaded my way through them till I found the well-worn path that brought me back, at last, to the riverside.

GRANTCHESTER MEADOW
ON
THE RIVER CAM
CAMBRIDGE

AND
11/24/19

For the next forty-five minutes or so I was Samwise Gamgee, ambling along that low, quiet river through sunlit fields of cattle, under the shady boughs of willows and chestnuts whose limbs draped lovingly over the river. Soon the path veered away from the river and across a field to the Orchard Tea Garden, where posh Brits sipped and chortled. Now I was in the village of Grantchester, famous partly for the BBC mystery series of the same name, but especially for the war poet Rupert Brooke. My head full of stories, my heart full of gladness, I ate lunch alone at a pub called The Green Man and wrote in my journal. All was well with the world.

It was only later that I discovered the rich history of that very walk. Way back in the 1300s, Geoffrey Chaucer wrote of the area in The Canterbury Tales. Rupert Brooke, whom Yeats called "the handsomest young man in England," wrote these homesick lines about Grantchester Meadow before he died in World War I:

> Oh! there the chestnuts, summer through,
> Beside the river make for you
> A tunnel of green gloom, and sleep
> Deeply above; and green and deep
> The stream mysterious glides beneath,
> Green as a dream and deep as death.

Sylvia Plath's poem "Watercolor of Grantchester Meadows" pays tribute to the cows:

> It is a country on a nursery plate.
> Spotted cows revolve their jaws and crop

Red clover or gnaw beetroot
Bellied on a nimbus of sun-glazed buttercup.
Hedging meadows of benign
Arcadian green
The blood-berried hawthorn hides its spines with white.

The biggest surprise, though, was the Roger Waters–penned Pink Floyd song "Grantchester Meadows," which calls us to:

Hear the lark and harken to the barking of the dog fox
Gone to ground
See the splashing of the kingfisher flashing to the water
And a river of green is sliding unseen beneath the trees
Laughing as it passes through the endless summer,
Making for the sea

This, friends, is what happens when you don't build a subdivision or a shopping center over one of earth's lovely places, but instead honor it and open it up for people to really see. It's what happens when the owner of those cows, unafraid of a lawsuit, allows the occasional rambler. For *centuries* the place gets memorialized in song and story. It is experienced and cherished by people like me from faraway lands for its simple, timeless beauty. In this way we give the place a chance to speak, and it insists that we acknowledge its sacredness, it's *place-ness*, which leads to both our sharing of it and our caring for it. (No great shock that I didn't see a single household appliance in the River Cam.)

As I keep saying, Mill Creek, a short walk from The Warren, is just as pretty—or it could be, that is, if we could see it from the greenway, if we let people walk along its banks and through the meadows, all the way to the village pub (which doesn't exist because of zoning regulations).

Because we're so entrenched in our way of life, our way of thinking about private land, it's going to be hard to change things. Until we do, the most beautiful parts of this great country will stay hidden away, unseen and unloved by anyone but the owners, and the succeeding generations will continue to think of the land as "mine" or "yours," and not "ours." That's not to say there aren't many fine things about America, this land of my sojourn. I'm going to keep loving it, and whenever people say the land is prettier on the other side of the sea, I'll stick up for it and remind them that the beauty here is just as deep—much of it is just hidden for now. Hidden beauty, it must be said, is better than no beauty at all.

So what is there to do but begin the patient work of hallowing what we have? This afternoon I planned to mow the front field, but my five-gallon gas can was empty. I drove to the gas station, by way of the Valley of Mordu and Dan's Crest, and on the way home I looked, as I always do, at the creek as I crossed the Mill Creek bridge. The water was high enough from yesterday's rain to kayak it, so I decided against mowing, called my brother, and insisted that he come out on the water with me. By the time he got to my house the sun was low in the sky, so when we were finally in the water the magic hour was upon us. The trees were aglow with it. As we floated through that quiet world of wonder, we heard the joggers and walkers on the greenway, just above us through the thick brush. They had no idea we were there, and probably didn't even think about the fact that just a few feet away an age-old waterway carried on as it has for thousands of years.

CANE RIDGE, TN 12-26-19   MILL CREEK   ANDK

When I got home, convicted by the writing of this chapter, I wrote a poem. I also asked a few neighbors to join me in the work of un-desecrating the creek, and offer here what are (as far as I know) the first published poems about this lovely gift that wends through the tall trees of Cane Ridge.

MILL CREEK IN SEPTEMBER
by Andrew Peterson

My brother and I took to the creek,
Two small boats, plying the golden hour.
Dodging wet stones at angles oblique,

FOOTPATHS

We listened to nearby walkers speak
Above the bank and beyond the bower.

Our presence unknown, our course unseen,
We glode well below the world they knew
In our world of water and rushes green,
Where oak limb bowed to the heron queen
As kingfishers, courting, swooped and flew.

Limestone embankments bordered and gleamed
Where spring water trickled over moss,
And sang its tune as the late sun streamed
Its light through leaves until it beamed
On lordly sycamores stretched across.

And in the end, we left it behind.
The sun left, too, and now the warm night
Envelops the valley, strikes us blind.
But I see the water in my mind,
Down below the bank in dark delight.

SUMMER STORM OVER MILL CREEK
(JULY 20, 2020)
by Shigé Clark

The water transforms.
Beneath the bridge, it swells—not like
a heart might, but like
lungs.

GOD OF THE GARDEN

Around the southward bend,
the Susans blink their brown eyes in the rain,
bashful beside bolder blackberries. The
bobbing globules smack
green from the ground and
send the scent of earth
into the trees.

They applaud—
oak and catalpa, elder boxer and dogwood
crowd the waterline to
watch. The patter pattern
breaking on their hands
like the tears of a man
too moved for speech, they bow
over bush and brush. Leaves
like pressed jewels gleam pied
on winding pavement. They have given
the air their richness.

Water wrenches the beauty out
and heaves it up to hang around us, leaves
it mist-wrapped to astound us,
sends the sun back rippling
rain-bowed over hay-heavy fields,
transforms.

Not like
a chisel might, but like
truth.

SOMETHING WILD
by Pete Peterson

Something wild was here,
 and something wild remembers
        still
the quiet trees bent down on knees
to drink the silent stream.
And they tell each other in the
rattle of leaves of a
wild as deep as their griefs.

The playing of rain,
        new with the fall,
                on crags of stone,
                        old since the Fall,
caresses the face of the aged rock
till he cracks a broken smile.
And he watches and mourns
the wild that was and
The wild that is,
        yet
he longs for the Wild to come.
For the wild is two-
        personed, split
into facets that shine out different lights.

The one the peace that undergirds creation,
building up and wearing down
but patient in the years;

and the other
    the careening thoughtlessness
    that surmounts the ancient stream,
        cuts
    the thoughtful hill,
    making straight the way
    that feet once knew by tip-toe
    round the ruminant roll of the land.

    That wildness breaks the trees
    that bent and shuddered,
    and mutters over the trouble of the
    babbling brook. But

when the night fights back the
cutting,
    rutting,
        wilder ways
and calls out the kingdom of
cadent cicada scream,
the groan of the wild,
resolves and
remembers—

that when the ungoverned falseness
speaking in the rattle of engines recedes,
The wildness of time will be gone, gone,
echoing into the fullness of a wilder peace,
untamed for then unbound,

when Wild itself shall overmaster wild,
and its ancient limbs limn the ancient hymn
    singing
        something
            Wild is near..

X

THE WEEPER IN THE TREES

The Clouds that gather round the setting sun
Do take a sober colouring from an eye
That hath kept watch o'er man's mortality.
—William Wordsworth

I won't go into what brought me there, to the frozen forest at dawn. It's enough to know that my heart was in turmoil, and I was angry at God. I was angry at him for his immense, oppressive silence—what felt like mute indifference in the face of his child's weeping anguish. Again and again I had cried out for relief, but received only more anguish. I was twenty-eight years old, exhausted, and scared to death of life.

One night, in what would be a foreshadowing of the janitor's closet many years later, I ended up in our bedroom closet, on my knees and wailing for help. It wasn't the first time, nor the last. I was desperate for healing, convinced that he was the healer, but Jesus was surrounded by the crowd and I couldn't press through. Oh, how I reached, stretched, clawed my way through the dirt, but the tips of my fingers couldn't touch him. Why, if he loved me so much, would he taunt me with the hem of his robe, dangling it just out of reach? Why wouldn't he fix what was broken? I experienced a shift from pain to anger, anger upwelling like tar from my soul's ragged valleys, anger that spilled out of my mouth as a whispered "I hate you" aimed at Love Himself. In a mindless fit of rage I slugged the wall with the side of my fist, and realized with a sick sort of glee that I had broken through the drywall.

After that, I slumped to the floor and lay motionless until some friends showed up and helped me out into the light, prayed for me, promised to call the next day. To be honest, I was terrified. I had never told God that I hated him before. I'd expressed disappointment, frustration, even anger—but I'd never used the word *hate*. All these years later, the memory still unsettles me. The next day I called a friend and shamefully told him what I'd said. "God can take it," was his reply. "Don't be afraid."

I was reassured that I hadn't forfeited my soul, but even so, a deadness seeped through me and into my day, suggesting that some kind of peace needed to be made. I didn't know how to make it, nor was I sure I wanted to just yet. As I've said before, very seldom have I struggled to believe in God. The struggle for me, when it comes, has always been believing that he's good. Were his intentions for me good? Would a good father respond to his child's anguish with silence? I decided to give him a taste of his own medicine. It proved difficult, however, to exist with properly working lungs, married to a lovely wife, father to healthy children, with food to eat and work to do, and yet to withhold silent thanks at every turn. I missed being able to talk to him, to bring him my questions and my small moments of delight, even in the midst of that season of pain. I was stubborn.

Finally, the friend who helped me out of the darkness of that bedroom closet told me, "Every year I go on a silent retreat at this monastery in Kentucky. It's this weekend. You should take my place. You need it worse than I do."

"But it's your name on the list," I said, trying to wiggle my way out of it.

"Doesn't matter. Just tell them you're me."

The mischievous pastor's kid in me got excited about the prospect of lying to monks, so I accepted. The closer the weekend got, the more nervous I became. Growing up a dyed-in-the-wool Protestant meant that I was unfamiliar with monasteries and what exactly one was supposed to do there. Would I have to don a robe? Shave my head? Hoe in the garden? All I knew for sure was that, according to my friend, many of the Trappists had taken vows of silence. God had given me the silent treatment, so I was eager to repay in kind. Maybe if I went to the trouble of driving all that way, spent my days fasting, read enough Scripture, and wrote enough in my journal, God would condescend to explain himself. Maybe I would "hear from the Lord," like all those other Christians seemed to do.

It was cold and dark when I left. It got colder as I drove north. The whole three-hour drive there my mind played tricks on me. Doubts rained down, temptations grew like weeds. Just a few exits before the one for the monastery I saw, illuminated by chilling artificial light, one of those roadside adult emporiums, and it seemed that all the demons in hell were chanting, coaxing me to pull over and sully my imagination while I had the chance. I defied the dark, unpleasant voices and fought my way ahead to exit 81, for Sonora—which literally means "pleasant sounding." I steered my car into the dark wooded hills, closer and closer to the oldest Trappist monastery in America and farther from the impersonal highway and its attendant seductions.

I had never read anything by Thomas Merton, so it was lost on me at the time that one of America's greatest writers had lived and written at the Abbey of Gethsemani. Many years later, I read his memoir, *The Seven Storey Mountain*, and was struck by how similar my arrival there was to his in 1941.

I looked at the rolling country, and at the pale ribbon of road in front of us, stretching out as grey as lead in the light of the moon. Then suddenly I saw a steeple that shone like silver in the moonlight, growing into sight from behind a rounded knoll. The tires sang on the empty road, and, breathless, I looked at the monastery light that was revealed before me as we came over the rise. At the end of an avenue of trees was a big rectangular block of buildings, all dark, with a church crowned by a tower and a steeple and a cross: and the steeple was as bright as platinum and the whole place was as quiet as midnight and lost in the all-absorbing silence and solitude of the fields. Behind the monastery was a dark curtain of woods, and over to the west was a wooded valley, and beyond that a rampart of wooded hills, a barrier and a defence against the world.

And all over the valley smiled the mild, gentle Easter moon, the full moon in her kindness, loving this silent place.[14]

I parked my car, grabbed my backpack, and walked in the dark silence to the porter's door. Now at last was my chance to lie to a monk. I was thrilled, and nervous, and eager to see what would happen. What I didn't know was that monks follow the Rule of St. Benedict, which champions hospitality for travelers. With relief and a bit of disappointment I saw a sign near the door, chiseled in stone, "Let all guests that come be

---

14. Thomas Merton, *The Seven Storey Mountain: An Autobiography of Faith* (1948, repr., New York: Harcourt, 1999), 350–51.

received like Christ." I didn't need to lie, it turned out. I just needed to seek and knock.

Here, Merton's story is exactly—and eerily—like my own, down to the brother's greying, pointed beard.

> I could hear someone stirring inside.
>
> Presently the key turned in the door. I passed inside. The door closed quietly behind me. I was out of the world.
>
> The effect of that big, moonlit court, the heavy stone building with all those dark and silent windows, was overpowering. I could hardly answer the Brother's whispered questions.
>
> I looked at his clear eyes, his greying, pointed beard. . . .
>
> We crossed the court, climbed some steps, entered a high, dark hall. I hesitated on the brink of a polished, slippery floor, while the Brother groped for the light switch. . . .
>
> We began to climb the wide stairs. Our steps echoed in the empty darkness. One flight and then another and a third and a fourth. There was an immense distance between floors; it was a building with great high ceilings. Finally we came to the top floor, and the Brother opened the door into a wide room, and put down my bag, and left me.
>
> I heard his steps crossing the yard below, to the gate house.

And I felt the deep, deep silence of the night, and of
peace, and of holiness enfold me like love, like safety.
The embrace of it, the silence! I had entered into
a solitude that was an impregnable fortress. And the
silence that enfolded me, spoke to me, and spoke louder
and more eloquently than any voice, and in the middle
of that quiet, clean-smelling room, with the moon
pouring its peacefulness in through the open window,
with the warm night air, I realized truly whose house
that was . . .[15]

For me, the night air was cold, but that was the only difference from Merton's account. I was embraced by the living
silence of the place, and lay there long into the night, unable
to sleep.

I spent the next three days in my cell, leaving only to
listen from a balcony, with other guests, to the monks singing
vespers. I went to the library for a while, but felt oddly exposed
and returned to the womb of my quarters for the remainder
of my time. By the third morning, I had moved beyond the
romance of the silence and entered the familiar territory of
frustration again. The silence, which at first seemed like a kind
of answer, again became the silence of unanswered questions.
The white whale of my pain continued to breach, and I hurled
harpoon after harpoon at it, in very real danger of becoming
entangled in the ropes of my own rage. If I had stayed longer,
a lifetime perhaps, the pain would have been subsumed in that

---

15. Merton, *The Seven Storey Mountain*, 351–52.

ocean of stillness—but I only had three days, and then it was back to the only life I knew, out of the Sabbath woods of the monastery without the luxury of timeless devotion to a God who is slow to speak.

Still unable to sleep well in that unsettling quiet, I climbed out of the cot on the last day a little before dawn and stole to the frigid parking lot with my bag. The experiment was nice, I thought, but ultimately it was another foiled attempt at gaining audience with the King. All questions, no answers. All mystery, no revelation. What more did he want from me? Fasting, praying, and waiting were apparently not enough. I threw my bag in the trunk and shut it a little too hard, the sound echoing across the monastery grounds in the breathless dawn. I glanced across the street at that "dark curtain of woods" and saw a small white sign staked into the ground. Moving closer, I made out the words, "To the Statues," next to an arrow that pointed to a footpath leading into the shadowy enclosure of trees.

I cupped my hands and breathed into them for warmth, looking from my car to the path and back again. Driven by curiosity, I locked the car (ridiculously, since the monks probably had no use for my stereo), and stepped out of one world and into another. It's easy to miss if you're not thinking about it, so next time you enter a stand of trees, pay attention to the way the air changes. The sound is muffled, and yet for reasons I don't understand the trees echo when you call into them. Birds flit from branch to branch as if flustered that you'd have the audacity to enter their house uninvited. Whereas before you could only feel the wind, now you can see it, brushing the overstory, going where it pleases. In freezing temperatures at sunrise, all these effects are heightened, and one is acutely aware of one's own intrusion on a sacred stillness. The only thing quite like it is stepping from a city street into an airy cathedral.

Hands stuffed deep into the pockets of my coat, I followed the path through silent sentinels of dormant trees, climbing hills, then descending into hollows, wondering what the statues would be. Deep into the woods I discovered a rickety shack and poked my head inside. There was a notebook and a pen, where pilgrims had written prayers. I read some, and felt a little ashamed for eavesdropping on the cries of so many hearts. Breathing on my fingers again to get the blood flowing, I took up the pen and poured my lonely heart onto the page, crying real tears and getting uncomfortably specific in spite of the fact that anyone at all could read my most private agonies. I don't remember exactly what I wrote, but it amounted to this:

Help me. God, please. I'm not mad anymore, but I need you. Help me.

By now the dawn had lightened to daybreak, and I wanted to go home. I missed Jamie and the kids. I had come this far, had given up my fight and broken my silence with God, and was deeply cold. I looked back the way I had come, then spotted another sign, repeating the invitation: *to the statues.* A breath of wind stirred the upper branches. On I walked, deeper into the lonely trees, asking again and again, "Where are you? Why won't you answer?"

At last, the trail banked to the right and I was presented with a sculpture of three men, huddled together in sleep.

It took a moment, but I realized it was a depiction of Peter, James, and John, unable to keep watch with Jesus on the night he was betrayed. This was the Abbey of Gethsemani, of course, a whole monastery named after the night Jesus went to the woods to pray. So I knew what was next. I followed the footpath ahead and the clutch of trees opened into a small clearing.

Dead in the center, frozen in the gray light, was the statue of a man in a state of desperation. This was no classical, pietistic display of a barely human Christ. No, this was different. He looked to have stumbled to his knees. His back was arched, his head thrown back. His hands covered his face so that his elbows were splayed out. His friends were asleep, and all the dormant trees were sleeping, too. Not even his own creation kept watch with him that morning, as he knelt in the terrible silence of that lonesome forest. Then I, too, fell to my knees and wept, wanting, strangely, to comfort *him*, to tell him he wasn't alone, that I had walked through a freezing wilderness to be with him, that I would keep watch, dear master. With a gust, the knowledge swept into me that I knew my savior better in the silence than I had ever known him in the song. Ah, Lord, how precious is your weeping presence with those who weep! How much better is your companionship in the deep darkness than your absence in the light! I was not alone. I had never been alone. My own descent into the dark woods of desolation was merely a footpath to the heart of Christ—Christ, who went to the grove to pray; Christ, who asked his friends to keep watch with him; Christ, who in his anguish turned his face not away from the Father but *to* him, who aimed his questions at the silent dome of heaven and got an angry mob for an answer.

I also went to the woods for an answer, and found Jesus. I demanded words, and was given instead the silent, weeping Word that echoes in the lonely wood of every sorrowful heart, the Word all the books in the world cannot contain. In the dark night of my soul, he was the friend who kept watch.

I wish I could say that my encounter with Christ at the Abbey of Gethsemani was the end of my suffering, but it wasn't. There were months, years of healing ahead. But it's no exaggeration to say that I never forgot the resounding truth that the Son is present in the silence of the desolate wood, the Spirit moves the branches of those leafless trees, and the Father looks on with a gentle patience.

Not long after I got home, I wrote "The Silence of God."

It's enough to drive a man crazy
It'll break a man's faith
It's enough to make him wonder
If he's ever been sane
When he's bleating for comfort
From thy staff and thy rod
And the heavens' only answer
Is the silence of God

It'll break a man's timbers
When he loses his heart
When he has to remember
What broke him apart

This yoke may be easy
But this burden is not
When the crying fields are frozen
With the silence of God

And if a man has got to listen
To the voices of the mob
Who are reeling in the throes
Of all the happiness they've got
When they tell you all their troubles
Have been nailed up to that cross,
Well, then, what about the times
When even followers get lost
'Cause we all get lost sometimes

There's a statue of Jesus
On a monastery knoll
In the hills of Kentucky
All quiet and cold
And he's kneeling in the garden
As silent as a stone
And all his friends are sleeping
And he's weeping all alone

And the man of all sorrows
Never forgot
What sorrow is carried
By the hearts that he bought
So when the questions dissolve

Into the silence of God
The aching may remain
But the breaking does not

The aching may remain
But the breaking does not
In the holy, lonesome echo
Of the silence of God

I've only been back to the Abbey once in all these years. But every time I pass exit 81 and see the word "Sonora," I am reminded of the pleasing sound of God's silence filling those woods. It is a pregnant silence, the silence of sleeping trees, the silence of winter at dawn. It can be a sound of pleading, too, of courageous submission to the will of the Father—and what may begin as submission becomes mission with each weary step: *proclaim the deeds of the Lord.* We enter the forest with a heavy burden, and emerge from it with a burden and a brother. I have wandered far, but he has never left me.

I love him, that weeper in the trees.

XI

PLACES AND NO-PLACES

On the north bank of Mill Creek, there are eighty-six acres for sale. I'd buy it tomorrow if I had a spare three million bucks lying around. It's zoned residential, with the potential for commercial development, which understandably has us Cane Ridgers hot and bothered; the last thing any of us wants is a Dollar General sprouting like a noxious weed in the middle of the valley. I often describe Cane Ridge as "Nashville, with cows." It's one of the last pockets of Davidson County where, in the Valley of Mordu for instance, one can still see things the way they would have been a century ago, with herds of sleek cattle chewing the cud beside a pond. We love being close enough to town to take in a movie or a concert at the Ryman, close enough to be a part of the vibrant cultural life of a good city, and yet far enough away that there's a measure of privacy and a reason to care for the land. I used to think that to have the one, you had to forsake the other, but my mind has changed over the years. Few things are more wonderful to me than a graceful integration of nature and culture, which is essentially what a garden is—and few things are less wonderful to me than the razing of a forest to plaster yet another soulless subdivision onto yet another corner of the land.

Because Cane Ridge is one of the last bastions of farmland left in Nashville, it's the kind of place real estate developers drool over. They snap up a bunch of acreage, bulldoze it to oblivion, subdivide it into tiny lots, and sell it off quick at a hefty profit, often without the developer ever setting foot on the land. For the last few hundred years in America, land has been seen not as a civic good, something we all get to share and steward, but primarily as a way to get rich. There's just so much of it here—miles upon miles of land stretching all the way to the Pacific, and that lack of scarcity has led to a lack of care.

KINGSCROFT MEADOW   11/27/20

It's true that people need places to live, and I don't begrudge anyone the dream of owning a pretty house for their kids to grow up in—but I believe we need more than just houses. We need *homes*, and a home is more than just the four walls where we eat and sleep and watch Netflix. It's a place that shapes and gives meaning to our lives. We need Places with a capital P, places that honor the community's history, the sacredness of creation, and our basic human need for beauty and nature. But we have become, according to James Howard Kunstler, a country of "no-places." I don't agree with everything he says in his book *The Geography of Nowhere*, but I agree with enough to commend it to you. There are essentially three kinds of places in America: the city, the country, and that weird in-between thing we call the suburbs. Ah, the suburbs: that slice of America where we name subdivisions after the trees we've cut down to build them, where we've zoned out any hope of a bookstore or a restaurant within walking distance, where we slave over lawns that we seldom use, where our front porches are too shallow for a porch swing, where we walk the dogs but can't walk to lunch, where we don't really get to know the neighbors because nobody's planning to stick around for more than a few years, where the dominant feature of every house is the two-car garage door, where getting to know people is tougher than it needs to be because there's no village pub, no local bakery, no farmer's market—in other words, no casual gathering point where it's possible to bump into neighbors in an organic way.

I realize it's likely that most of the people reading this book live in (and enjoy living in) something like I've just described, and I may have just lost you. But allow me to back away and gesture placatingly as you reach for your rotten tomatoes, reminding you with nervous laughter that I also lived for years in a subdivision and have to drive through one now to get to The Warren. I speak from experience. Like you, I once perused the aisles of Lowe's for the best grass seed and strove to out-green my neighbor's lawn. I also went to HOA meetings and voted to re-mulch the playground in the common area. I also went on morning walks with the baby stroller and grumbled when cars blocked the sidewalk. And yet I have come to think of subdivisions as "no-places." They're communities with no commerce, sidewalks that lead to no real destination, town-less clusters of houses and more houses, places without Place.

But it's not just subdivisions. It's also shopping districts surrounded by literal acres of asphalt parking lots. The same fast-food restaurants abound, along with the same coffee chains, the same department stores, the same facades, the same traffic congestion, the same, same sameness whether you're in Portland, Maine or Portland, Oregon; Jacksonville, Florida or Jackson, Tennessee. As I've said, as a traveling musician, it's comforting to be able to find a Chipotle or a Target when you need one, no matter where you are. The convenience of ubiquity, to be sure, is alluring. But when I get home from one of those trips, I seldom tell Jamie how wonderful this or that place was because it might as well have been five miles from our house—unless I really go out of my way to find the downtown, or the city parks, or use Wikipedia to discover what, if anything, makes the town unique.

To be clear, I'm not bashing America. This country, as I've said, is brimming with history, with beauty, with Place-ness. I've walked the riverside in St. Charles, Missouri, where Lewis and Clark embarked on their voyage to the West. I've mean-dered the walkways along the Reedy River in Greenville, South Carolina. I've marveled at the fish, fruit, and flowers at Pike Place Market in Seattle and jogged through the history of old Richmond, Virginia. I've walked through the resurrected down-towns of Chattanooga, Tennessee, and Montgomery, Alabama. It's not the cities with their garden parks, bustling centers, and walkable boroughs that I struggle to love. Nor, for that matter, is America's wilderness difficult to love, from the Grand

Canyon to the Everglades to the Blue Ridge Mountains. No, my beef is with the in-betweens, the no-places, the suburban sprawl—which is where many of us live out our days.

I've done quite a bit of reading on how we got here (Kunstler's *The Geography of Nowhere*, Jane Jacobs's towering *The Death and Life of Great American Cities*, and Eric Jacobsen's *Sidewalks in the Kingdom*, to name a few), and, like the history of England's footpaths, it's a complicated issue that I don't pretend to fully understand. I can, however, testify as a practitioner (so to speak) of America's cities, because over the years I've visited all fifty states—walking, driving, flying, eating, and conversing in all manner of cultures and subcultures.

A few years ago I was in a van with my friend Caleb on the way to a show, driving down a stretch of road somewhere in the South. He looked out the window and said something like, "I'm always glad to get off the interstate, because it reminds me that this," he gestured at a subdivision, followed by another subdivision, followed by a wasteland of downed trees that were about to become a subdivision, "is most of America. It's not the cities. It's this." I'd never thought of it like that before, but I'm inclined to agree. Somewhere along the way, someone had the idea to create neighborhoods out of thin air, make all the houses more or less the same, zone them so there was no town or city life within walking distance, and market them as the culmination of the good life. We put the parks a few miles over there, the shopping a few miles over that way, work way over yonder, and trusted that cars would get us where we needed to go.

A few years ago Jamie and I were in the Yorkshire Dales, and we parked in a village to grab some lunch at a pub. I grabbed my trusty Ordnance Survey map and suggested that we go on a walk after our pot pie, so Jamie and I climbed the hill past the shops and the old stone cottages, winding through the village's narrow streets to find the gate that opened like a portal to the countryside. We walked for a few miles, past the ruins of Iron Age settlements, through plantings of birch trees, down into green, grassy valleys and up onto windswept moors. Over the course of a few hours we passed several other walkers. One of them called out from a rise in the land several yards ahead, "Do you like wildflowers?"

"Of course," I answered.

She said, "If you're going this way, keep your eye out for the fen violets down to the right. I've never seen so many before."

About that time a man crested the hill, waved at us, and said, "So many violets! Just lovely." He asked us where we were from, and we talked about his travels in America. "It's a beautiful country," he said. "But have you noticed that you always have to drive somewhere to get into the countryside? I've never understood that. Here, you can just walk straight from town into this." He gestured at the spread of green hills and stone fences. "I spend hours out here every week, and it never gets old."

To this day, I've never had a conversation with a fellow American about a profusion of wildflowers just around the bend. I'm not saying it doesn't happen, just that it's never happened to me. The violets, by the way, were pretty, but a bit anticlimactic. When we saw them, the other walkers' excitement seemed a bit disproportionate. But upon reflection I was charmed by their delight in so small a thing. Their eyes were peeled, they saw a quiet beauty, and they wanted to share the news. The point is, there wasn't a vast distance between the life of the town and the life of the country. They were butted up against each other and each was improved by the nearness of the other.

That brings me back to that eighty-six-acre lot in Cane Ridge. As I said, there's a greenway along our stretch of Mill Creek which connects several neighborhoods, with Lennox Village at one end and Orchard Bend park and its soccer fields at the other. Because of Nashville's vibrant community of immigrants, you'll see all manner of peoples, tribes, and tongues out there walking dogs and pushing strollers. I love it. But it's nigh impossible to get to know anyone because there's no gathering point, no natural way to share life together. I'm sure that as I write this, developers are eyeing Google Maps and crunching numbers, evaluating their backend if they were to buy the land, down all the trees, split it up, and sell it off as yet another subdivision.

There's a term for the kind of land I'm describing: *infill*. Not farmland. Not forest. Not an ecosystem of wildlife and natural features. Just infill. A blank space on a schematic to be filled in with whatever makes someone the most money. It breaks my heart. Just a few miles down the road some friends lived on the oldest remaining farm in Davidson County, and it had the distinction of being designated a "century farm," meaning it had been in continuous agricultural production for more than a hundred years. They eventually sold it for what I'm sure were good reasons, and the developers are even now hard at work hauling away every tree, scraping every last scrap of that farm from the earth in order to make a new commercial development. I feel a physical ache every time I pass it. In a fit of painful irony, the developers named what is now a wasteland of bulldozers and blasting zones "Century Farms." I actually know one of the folks who closed the deal, and he's a great guy—but business is business, and that lovely old homestead was standing in the way. Now all I can do is hope they develop it into something beautiful and good for the community, and to be fair, they just might.

But the acreage along Mill Creek is almost literally in my front yard—I can see it from the porch—so I'm desperate to save it somehow. I've called friends who are developers and pleaded with them. I literally hold out my hand every time I drive past it and pray, "Lord, please let whoever buys this property turn it into something good for this community." Let it be a garden park along the creek, with benches and wildflower meadows and places to picnic. Let it be a place where all these varied people can come together and learn to live in love and not fear. Let human culture elevate, not denigrate, what God has made here. Let there be places to eat, places to work, places to grow things. Let Cane Ridge be more than a place to be haphazardly infilled but a place that is full of life—a place with a story. That's really what I'm getting at. We need stories; stories need places. Places need people, and people need homes. We were made for community, but so many things about this in-between world of no-places seem designed to hinder it instead. The absence of commerce means walking is merely for fresh air, with no real destination. It means there's no place to casually bump into your neighbors. The absence of commerce means strangers are scarce. That leads to a fear of strangers, and the presence of fear is an absence of love. Jane Jacobs points out that in cities, crime actually goes up in the nicer neighborhoods with no commerce and therefore fewer people. Think about it. If you were walking in a bustling farmer's market, then you turned down a street where you were alone but for one other person, would you feel more or less comfortable?

There is, of course, a theological component to all this, and Eric Jacobsen writes about it well in *Sidewalks in the Kingdom*. In essence, he demonstrates that the way we shape our cities, towns, infrastructure, and homes is a reflection of what we believe to be true about human flourishing (and creation's flourishing) as children of God. Are we meant to live so much of our lives in automobiles? Are we meant to mainly consume food that was grown or processed a thousand miles away? Are we meant to only experience the wonder of creation in a national park, once a year, after a four-hour drive on holiday, or could we perhaps experience it on a walk after lunch thanks to the discovery of a field of wild violets? Are we meant to spend more time in the bonus room with the flat-screen than the front garden? These are good questions, and I believe Jacobsen gives us good answers.

My friend Matt Canlis is a pastor in Washington State. He studied under Eugene Peterson, who told him that he should travel to the United Kingdom and learn how to be a pastor in a small parish. Matt and his wife, Julie, moved to Scotland for grad school and lived in a Scottish village for several years. Matt made a short film called *Godspeed* about what he learned during his time there. There's a certain romance to it, but it wasn't at all easy. In the film Matt describes his first day on the job at the church. He asked the senior pastor where his office would be, and the bemused pastor replied, "Office?" Then he walked Matt outside and showed him the church sign, on which was written the pastor's home phone number. He waved a hand at the village and said, "This is your office. Get to know the people." Thus began Matt's education of living a life at "God's speed." Jesus, other than when he rode a donkey's colt, apparently walked everywhere he went. He had time to spot the wildflowers, converse with his friends, and experience a culture built to human (and not automobile) scale. He lived his life at three miles per hour. If you haven't seen *Godspeed*, I implore you to watch online and try to apply its wisdom to your life right here, right now.[16] I've talked to quite a few people who used to live overseas, and when I ask them what they miss the most about it, the answer is almost always, "I miss walking. Walking to the grocery store. Walking to church. Walking to the coffee shop."

Of course, even in the most idyllic walkable community, people are still broken. The world is still broken. If I could snap my fingers and add a café and a bookstore to every subdivision in America (and oh, how I wish I could!), there would still be deep-rooted problems underfoot. But if we integrated the loveliness of creation with the flourishing of human culture

---

16. https://www.livegodspeed.org/watchgodspeed-cover

would we be that much closer to a vision of the New Creation? I think we would. The story of redemption ends with a tree and a river *in* a city. In other words, the New Jerusalem will be not just a marriage of heaven and earth, but a marriage of nature and culture. Tim Keller has written at length about the goodness of cities, and in *Surprised by Hope* N. T. Wright casts a vision of Christians at work in the public square, in the planning of equitable communities, in the proper stewardship of natural resources, as a way of living as resurrection people serving the reigning King of heaven and earth.

We might as well get started by thinking of our neighborhoods as places, not no-places. Get into the neighborhood on foot, at God's speed. Keep your eyes peeled for the fen violets, and for image-bearing children of God scattered across your path, too. Let the American dream be supplanted by one of the Kingdom, where every square inch of the earth belongs to Jesus and we shape our sidewalks and streets, our homes, farms, and restaurants accordingly.

And if you're a developer and you're reading this, do me a favor and start with Cane Ridge.

It's so much more than "infill."

XII

A STONE'S THROW FROM JERUSALEM

Thanks to the human heart by which we live,
Thanks to its tenderness, its joys, and fears,
To me the meanest flower that blows can give
Thoughts that do often lie too deep for tears.
—William Wordsworth

In downtown Stockholm, the *Gamla Stan* (the "Old City") is a breathtaking maze of narrow and winding cobbled streets, with buildings painted in soft earth tones, regal statues, and shops selling everything from gelato to replicas of Viking swords. It's a little touristy in places, but since I'm a tourist I don't mind. My first time there I happened upon a place that sells old maps and prints, arranged by region. I went straight to the section labeled Småland—literally, "Small Land," which is the wooded, rural south of the country—where my great-grandfather was born. Before that first trip I had called Dad to ask about where our ancestors lived, and I heard him humming to himself on the other end of the line as he rustled the papers of his family history file. "It says here that your grandfather's dad, Ernest, was born in a place called . . . Kalmar." *Kalmar.* I was so glad it was a solid, easy-to-pronounce name. (Side note: I loved the fantasy novel ring to it so much that one of the main characters in The Wingfeather Saga ended up with it. [Side note-side note: I eventually learned that Ernest was from a village outside of Kalmar named "Kindbäcksmåla," which I can still barely pronounce and would not have sounded nearly as heroic.])

Back to the map store. I found an 1840 etching of the Castle Kalmar that took my breath away. I stood there in the aisle gazing at a beautiful castle, with spired turrets at the corners, stout battlements, arrow slits, and a moat. The Baltic Sea stretched out behind it, and in the foreground a peasant led a cow through some trees. The picture had been drawn before the American Civil War, at least sixty years before my great-grandfather had come to the New World. This, I thought, is what it would have looked like when my great-grandfather was a boy. He was a farmer in Småland, he surely would have had reason to visit Kalmar, and this—*this* is what he saw. He grew up in a place with actual castles. I'm sure it was over-priced but I bought the picture anyway. It hangs on the wall of the Chapter House.

A few years later I got to do a show in Kalmar, so I took a picture of the print before I left home; I wanted to compare the artist's depiction to the real thing. My hosts put me up in a lovely inn just a few blocks from the castle, so after I checked in I went on a private stroll to see the place. On the way I passed through a beautiful old cemetery where I found a whole host of Peterson graves—which was cool but meant next to nothing, since there are a zillion Petersons in Sweden.

But then I got to the castle itself. It was just as beau-tiful as the 1840 picture suggested. I crossed the moat on a drawbridge, passed through the gate under a portcullis, and wandered the ramparts, gazing out past the parapets at the fussy Baltic Sea. This place I had only seen in my imagination (with the help of an artist's etching) was real. I was moving around inside the picture I had stared at for years. After my long stroll through the castle grounds, I went on a hunt for the exact place where the artist of my etching would have set up shop to draw it, mainly to see if the same trees were still there. Sure enough, near the gate house I found the spot, held up the picture, and there they were. The same copse of trees, triple the size now, their leafy branches forming a green tunnel just before the drawbridge. That meant my great-grandfather, and likely *his* father, had laid eyes on these very trees back before there were Volvos or IKEA stores. The collision of imagination and reality is a thrill, like when Edmund and Lucy tumble into the painting in *The Voyage of the Dawn Treader.*

Now, imagine that feeling of tumbling into a story—and multiply it by a thousand.

That's what it's like to visit Israel.

We got off the plane in Tel Aviv and took a bus to the Sea of Galilee. It was a simple as that. No magic wardrobe, no "second star to the right and straight on till morning." Just a plane from New York, then a diesel bus to a brain-bending world of wonder. That's what it was like for this pastor's kid from the other side of earth, anyway. That night in Tiberius a few of us threw on our bathing suits and went for a midnight dip in the Sea of Galilee, under wheeling stars, in the same waters where Peter fished, where Jesus slept in a storm and sauntered on the waves. Honestly, I've never felt anything quite so mentally stimulating in my life as the days I spent there. They call that land "holy" for good reason. I kept reminding myself that it wasn't a dream, or some intricate virtual reality simulation, but was as real as my kitchen counter. On the bus ride to Galilee, my friend Russ (who had lived in Israel years ago during seminary) pointed out the window and said, "Nazareth is a few miles over that way."

I looked out past the highway at a rocky wilderness that didn't look much different from anything else. "How do you know?"

"Because I've been there," he said with a shrug. "That's where it is."

Looking back, I see that I was still struggling to transpose the many maps I'd seen in the back of pew Bibles into three dimensions. It was so hard to believe we were *in* the map, viewing it not objectively from above, but on a highway driving west, so that Nazareth could just be, you know, "over there." It was the exact opposite of disorienting. All the stories that had populated my imagination suddenly took on flesh, and I dwelt among them. I would have been no less amazed if Russ had gestured out past the rolling hills and said, "Hobbiton is over there, just beyond Bree."

But this was *real*. We spent a few days in Galilee, from Peter's house in Capernaum to a newly excavated first-century synagogue in Madgdala (as in, "Mary Magdalene"), where Jesus would certainly have taught when he "went throughout Galilee, teaching in their synagogues" (Matt. 4:23). With the exception of the cities of Tiberius and Sepphoris, the whole area around the sea was agrarian in Jesus' day, which helps explain his near-constant use of earthy metaphors. In fact, the remains of the earliest known traces of cultivation on the planet are right there on the shores of Galilee. It's fascinating to me that

God chose to be born where, as far as we can tell, people have tilled the earth longer than anywhere else. High above the Sea of Galilee, on the side of a mountain where it's believed Jesus delivered the Sermon on the Mount, we read aloud that very passage, then spent some time wandering in meditation. I followed a trail down through the brush to a lonely place and discovered a modern stand of beehives. Have you ever considered the fact that there were beekeepers in Galilee? Honey is mentioned sixty-one times in Scripture, my favorite instance of which is after the resurrection, when the apostles offer Jesus broiled fish and honey. Yes, John the Baptist ate locusts and wild honey, but the fact that it's specified as "wild" suggests that there were apiaries, too.

We walked under the hot sun among fig, olive, acacia, and eucalyptus trees, gazing out at the ridgelines of the surrounding mountains. Many people complain that Israel is disappointing, overrun with tourists and dubious claims about where this or that happened. But as Henry Van Dyke (who composed the lyrics to the hymn "Joyful, Joyful We Adore Thee") wrote in *Out-of Doors in the Holy Land,*

> *Four things, I know, are unchanged amid all the changes that have passed over the troubled and bewildered land. The cities have sunken into dust: the trees of the forest have fallen: the nations have dissolved. But the mountains keep their immutable outline: the liquid stars shine with the same light, move on the same pathways: and between the mountains and the stars, two other changeless things, frail and imperishable,—the*

flowers that flood the earth in every springtide, and the
human heart where hopes and longings and affections
and desires blossom immortally.[17]

If you go, keep your eyes on the stars, the shape of the mountains, and the things that grow upon the earth, and it's a safe bet that your human heart will blossom with longings, affections, desires.

Of all the places God-in-flesh could have chosen to live, he decided on a little corner of creation where people farmed, kept bees, cultivated grapes, fished, walked footpaths, and lived in close community. He lived near to the earth, with an intimate awareness of the way things grew in their season, the way humans cultivated and cared for his creation. What delight he must have felt, knowing in his skin the feel of wood and stone and water, joining his children in the deep satisfaction of "making something of the world." He also, it must be said, loved the city—enough to grieve Jerusalem's coming destruction. So we left Galilee after a few days and "went up to Jerusalem," our bus laboring up the steep, stony mountains to the precious place that once contained the Holy of Holies, where David danced, where God was murdered, and where he conquered death.

Our hotel was just outside the walls of Old Jerusalem. We arrived late, so a few of us went on a midnight walk through the labyrinthine streets and passageways of one of earth's great cities. Again, my mind was stretching, superimposing all

---

17. Henry Van Dyke, *Out-of-Doors in the Holy Land: Impressions of Travel in Body and Spirit* (New York: Charles Scribner's Sons, 1920), 7–8.

the stories I knew over the paths we wandered in that warm night. It was almost too much to bear.

The next day was Friday, so sundown marked the start of the Sabbath. As the dusk deepened, we went to the Western Wall of the Temple Mount, which is the nearest the Jews can get to the site of the temple these days. Because it was the start of *Rosh Hashanah*, the Jewish new year, things were more intense than usual. We were told by our Jewish guide that we were welcome to approach the wall to pray, welcome to join with the weeping or the dancing, welcome to immerse ourselves in the wild wonder of the moment. "It is a very special day," he said with a smile. We entered the court, and all around me, men with long curls dangling in front of their ears, Scriptures open in their hands, all wearing long, flowing robes, chanted words of the prophets. I found an English translation and stood at the wall, joining them in their praise and their lament, in their longing for a new temple. Without having to try, all my heart's affections, desires, yearnings were drawn as if by a powerful magnet to the person of Jesus, through whom all things are made new. I placed one hand on the wall and allowed my imagination to blossom like those fields of wildflowers in Galilee. This was Mount Moriah, where Abraham was spared from sacrificing Isaac by the ram caught in the brambly tree. This was where Solomon completed the temple whose pillars were pomegranate trees, where the Ark of the Covenant rested—the same ark that contained the ten commandments, the manna, and, yes, a tree: Aaron's staff that had budded with new leaves. Not far away was the site where the crucifixion tree was planted atop Skull Hill, and not far away from that the Root of David, Abraham's seed, was planted and reborn in a garden. This was where, at Jesus' triumphant "It is finished!" the curtain was torn in two and he opened for us the gate of glory, which leads his children to a New Jerusalem where a Tree of Life will straddle the holy river. I was overwhelmed with love, and by love.

I stood in the eye of a storm made up of living stories. Stories were the wind and the rain and the rolling thunder, and Jesus was king of it all. The fourth and final book of The Wingfeather Saga was the most difficult to write, because like any author I was striving to tie up all the loose ends, to give some pleasing symmetry to the whole tale, so that the ending satisfies the reader by interlocking with the beginning. Nobody likes a story that doesn't hold together. So it was as a feeble storyteller that I stood with my hand on the wall that Sabbath evening, and was broken in worship, adoring with all of my soul the author of creation's epic—an epic held perfectly together in one shimmering knot we call Jesus. In all my life I've never longed for him more. I wanted to sing for him, to thank him for stepping into the map to lead his children home. When I was a young man I asked God to let me tell his story, to allow his child to proclaim the deeds of the Lord to the nations. I begged him for it anew as I wept at the Western Wall.

And yet.

The very next day I was plagued again with doubt and self-loathing, unable on a minute-by-minute basis to accept the plain fact that Jesus loves me, no matter how often the Bible tells me so. It's one thing to stand in awe before a holy king amidst the throng; it's another to be embraced by his incarnation, a small-town rabbi with callused hands and tender eyes. It's astonishing to me that, even after literal mountaintop experiences like that one in Jerusalem, I carry so much fear, such propensity for shame. The Western Wall gave me a fresh astonishment for God the Father, King of the Universe. But Jesus wasn't finished with me yet.

Our group drove to Bethlehem, and I looked out on the stony valley where the angels appeared in glory to the shepherds. Again and again, my own broken history presented itself to me, and I struggled to believe that this mighty God-made-man who suffered the little children to come unto him would suffer me, too.

A few years ago our church hosted a night of prayer and Scripture reading called *lectio divina* (literally, "divine reading"), in which you read a passage of Scripture four times, each time allowing words, phrases, or images that stand out to guide your prayers. The passage we read was the one in Matthew 19 where the disciples rebuke the people who bring their children to be blessed by Jesus. Jesus, of course, rebukes the rebukers, and welcomes the children. The pastor asked us, after a few readings, where we saw ourselves in that story. As I listened to other people's answers, my cheeks flushed and tears sprang to my eyes—because I pictured myself in that story as a little Illinois boy dragged from the wilds of Florida, a boy who had been stained by his own sins. I saw that boy hiding behind his parents' legs, afraid to be seen, as the other kids approached the gentle shepherd. That boy wants to be near Jesus, but his fear of rejection prevents him. The thought of those tender, brown eyes falling on him fills him with longing and terror in equal measure, so he struggles to hide, even as his parents nudge him forward. I wrote this Lenten Sonnet about it that night.

"Suffer the little children to come near,"
You say. But I hold back. My parents try.
Nudging, they hiss stern orders in my ear,
But my sandaled feet won't move. Petrified,
I balk as the others approach. You bless
Each of them in turn, placing your warm hand
On their heads, speaking kindly as they press
Forward, unafraid, eager just to stand
Near you. But I know my own wretched heart.
I know when you see me you'll know it too.
Your eyes see everything. You'll just depart
With a look of disappointment, won't you?
Don't look, Lord. Let me hide in this shadow.
You're too good. I'm too bad. But please—don't go.

That's how I felt after the Western Wall. In awe of God's glory, but from a safe distance. I wanted to behold, without being held. It was fine for God to see me as a map, but I was unspeakably frightened that he would enter my own landscape and wander the footpaths of my shattered hills. Please, Jesus, for now just let me wander the quiet wood of your goodness, seeing but unseen. Knowing what I know of him in the Gospels, it's unreasonable, but I carried in my chest a stone of dread that the bright gaze of love would fall on me, then move away in disgust.

But that was before we went to the trees.

We drove from Bethlehem to the Mount of Olives. From there, you get perhaps the most famous view of Jerusalem: the city walls, the Dome of the Rock, the Southern Steps, all that hewn stone glowing golden under a vivid blue sky. We snapped our pictures and laughed with delight at a nearby camel, then soberly watched a Jewish funeral, with mourners in black among all the white tombs that drifted like snow down to the Kidron Valley. I knew the Garden of Gethsemane was next, and prepared myself for the possibility that I would be unmoved. I knew it wasn't necessarily the same garden, after all. Two thousand years is a lot of time for things to change, so you have to allow the traditional spots to inform your imagination and not get too hung up on the specifics. And yet, it surely happened *somewhere* nearby, and that's something.

We walked a footpath down the mountain and entered the shady grove of ancient olive trees. Their stout trunks were gnarled, twisting upward to splayed branches. The little grayish leaves held still in the warm, windless air. Many people milled about, yet no one spoke above a murmur. The trees were surrounded by an iron fence, so I found a place to kneel, reached through, and felt the rough skin of a tree that had been growing there for a thousand years. I surreptitiously pulled a few leaves from a branch and slipped them into my pocket. After all the bustle of Jerusalem, the jolting bus rides, the constant nearness of people, I hadn't realized until that moment how much I missed trees: their quiet covering of leaves, their ageless and soothing presence.

The Warren came to mind, and I felt a tug in my heart for my wife and children so far away, for the woods full of hackberries and red cedars whose knots and low-slung limbs I knew so well. Whereas my imagination had been stretching with each new dimension of understanding for the whole of my time in Israel, the sudden familiar feel of a tree trunk produced an inrush of restful stillness. This was something I knew. My mind rested. I was reminded that, though I was far, far away, this was the same world as The Warren, and at once I was calmed by the generous serenity of leaf and branch, root and trunk. The towering God of the Western Wall seemed to remain across the valley like a pillar of fire, his presence thundering within the city walls, while in this little olive grove—even among the whispering crowd—I felt a blissful solitude: the silent gift of the Thinking Tree, the Big and Little Maples, the pecans at Shiloh, Warren Wood, the Enchanted Grove of oaks where the fawn wandered.

Still kneeling, one hand still on the olive tree, I opened my Bible and whispered Psalm 22 aloud—to myself, and to my God. I needed to remember his passion, the dread that drove him here, greatly troubled in spirit; here, where Jesus—the Root, the Seed, the True Vine, the Tree of Life—went among trees to pray to his Father.

As I read, Jesus made himself known in my own story. To be clear, I was in no way identifying my own suffering with his. It would be foolish to compare the worst of our human trials with the great darkness he endured, compounded by the physical and spiritual realms. The Blessing drank to the dregs the cup of the Curse. He who knew no sin *became* sin for us. It isn't that we suffer like him, but that he chose to suffer for us. He entered our death that we might enter his resurrection. In his agony, ours finds meaning and redemption; our pain is subsumed in the tidal wave of Christ's, and washes up clean on the shores of glory. It was under the olive boughs of Gethsemane that Jesus' gaze at last rested on the frightened little boy.

My God, my God, why have you forsaken me?
  Why are you so far from saving me,
    so far from my cries of anguish?
My God, I cry out by day, but you do not answer,
  by night, but I find no rest. (Ps. 22:1–2)

I remembered lying on my cot in the vast, stony silence of the monastery, tossing and turning, greatly troubled in spirit and unable to sleep.

Yet you are enthroned as the Holy One;
  you are the one Israel praises.
In you our ancestors put their trust;
  they trusted and you delivered them.
To you they cried out and were saved;
  in you they trusted and were not put to shame. (vv. 3–5)

In those long days of my soul's dark night, I sat in church as the saints sang hymns and felt the terrible loneliness of happy crowds. Why could I not join them? Why had they been rescued when I had not?

But I am a worm and not a man,
  scorned by everyone, despised by the people.
All who see me mock me;
  they hurl insults, shaking their heads.
"He trusts in the Lord*," they say,*
  "let the Lord *rescue him.*
Let him deliver him,
  since he delights in him." (vv. 6–8)

I thought of the taunting, demonic voices that fill my head with lies so loud I always believe them: "You are broken beyond repair. You break beyond repair everyone you love. The God you say you love could never love you, and if he could, he wouldn't bother."

> Yet you brought me out of the womb;
>> you made me trust in you, even at my mother's breast.
> From birth I was cast on you;
>> from my mother's womb you have been my God.
> (vv. 9–10)

My parents dressed me up on Sundays, led me across the gravel parking lot from the parsonage to the church. They impressed the words of Scripture on me and talked about them when they tucked me in, when they woke me for breakfast, when we walked the streets of Monticello to the Dairy Queen on the square.

> Do not be far from me,
>> for trouble is near
>> and there is no one to help.
> Many bulls surround me;
>> strong bulls of Bashan encircle me.
> Roaring lions that tear their prey
>> open their mouths wide against me.
> I am poured out like water,
>> and all my bones are out of joint. (vv. 11–14a)

I remembered punching the hole in the wall of my bedroom closet, and the bruise on the bones of my wrist the next morning. Oh, how the darkness cackled.

> My heart has turned to wax;
>> it has melted within me.
> My mouth is dried up like a potsherd,
>> and my tongue sticks to the roof of my mouth;
>> you lay me in the dust of death. (vv. 14b–15)

On the floor of the janitor's closet in North Carolina, I sobbed for hours, unable to lift myself from the floor. I was so thirsty my voice was gone, but I lacked the strength to rise.

> Dogs surround me,
>> a pack of villains encircles me;
>> they pierce my hands and my feet.
> All my bones are on display;
>> people stare and gloat over me.
> They divide my clothes among them
>> and cast lots for my garment. (vv. 16–18)

How can I not see you, precious Lord, hanging from the tree? How can I not shudder at the injustice of your terrible death?

> But you, LORD, do not be far from me.
>> You are my strength; come quickly to help me.
> Deliver me from the sword,
>> my precious life from the power of the dogs.

Rescue me from the mouth of the lions;
save me from the horns of the wild oxen. (vv. 19–21)

For all this, I have nowhere to turn but to you. When every friend has a stranger's face, and the pain is an unnameable cavity in my heart, when I stand alone in the night forest, my only consolation is the moon. From somewhere above and beyond, light spills down through the bony branches and draws my eyes to heaven. You, dear Jesus, knew the desperate pleading of the friendless night, and clung to the will of the Father.

I will declare your name to my people;
in the assembly I will praise you.
You who fear the LORD, *praise him!*
All you descendants of Jacob, honor him!
Revere him, all you descendants of Israel!
For he has not despised or scorned
the suffering of the afflicted one;
he has not hidden his face from him
but has listened to his cry for help. (vv. 22–24)

Love conquers slowly, like seedlings pushing through mud. It is only in hindsight that we see the broad, upwelling green of springtime as an explosion of life. Look back! He was always coming, always already there—

From you comes the theme of my praise in the great
assembly;
before those who fear you I will fulfill my vows.

The poor will eat and be satisfied;
　　those who seek the LORD *will praise him—*
　　may your hearts live forever! (vv. 25–26)

—and he was always going to be in the end, Lord of the Night, King of the Morning, Gardener of Oaks, Germinator, Tiller of the Heart's Soil, Reaper of the Glad Harvest. I was never abandoned, only furrowed by the Sower to bear good fruit. Get up, brother! Arise, sister! Go to the fields. Keep your promise. Ripen and rejoice.

All the ends of the earth
　　will remember and turn to the LORD,
and all the families of the nations
　　will bow down before him,
for dominion belongs to the LORD
　　and he rules over the nations.
All the rich of the earth will feast and worship;
　　all who go down to the dust will kneel before him—
　　those who cannot keep themselves alive.
Posterity will serve him;
　　future generations will be told about the Lord.
They will proclaim his righteousness,
　　declaring to a people yet unborn:
　　He has done it! (vv. 27–31)

I saw with new eyes what Christ has done, and why. I saw that he sees me, and he will not turn away. There in the olive grove, my fear was gone. His voice was clear and calm:

I love you.
Let me love you.

At last, I pushed through the parents clustered around the rabbi, rested my head on his warm lap, and wept as he laid his gentle hand on my head and spoke the blessing that was mine before he knit me in my mother's womb.

He has planted me and made me his own. Fed by the gentle waters of his Spirit, I beg him by faith to prune me as he will, to let me grow tall and broad, lit by the sun to bear his everlasting fruit unto the unending day of the New Creation.

And I will bear witness.

I will tell of his deeds.

EPILOGUE

It's winter. I hear a gusty wind in the night beyond the window, low and groaning like a distant jet plane, and it occurs to me that the trees are speaking. Their limbs are shaken and bent by the cold front tearing across Tennessee. The Chapter House is warm, with the embers of a tired fire crackling like morse code in the hearth beside me—again, the voice of trees. The temperature has been dropping all day, so the wooden bones of this little building are contracting, causing the wood-paneled ceiling to creak now and then. When I came in just now, shoulders up to my ears from the chill, I slammed the arch-top door a friend made out of reclaimed barn wood, rattling the wooden picture frames on the wall—one of them containing that eighteenth-century print of the Castle Kalmar (printed on wood-pulp, of course). I stomped my feet on the hardwood floor, and the trees spoke again.

The wooden shelves I built out of pine planks hold hundreds of books: Sayers, Chesterton, Lewis, and Tolkien; Wordsworth, Coleridge, Wilbur, Merton, and Berry. Trees made the pulp that made the pages (also known as leaves) where the words were preserved and printed and bound, each book the fruit of a life's labor. There are journals full of songwriting ideas: bad lines scratched out and reworked, furious scribblings, prayers preserved on paper. The walls around the drafting desk are covered with drawings made by wooden pencils (there's no smell quite like the aroma of pencil shavings dumped from the sharpener to the bin). Those drawings are mostly of trees, on sketch paper—again, made from trees. On the wooden mantel over the hearth there's a collection of old smoking pipes made from briar wood, one of which I bought in a busy tree-lined market in Bordighera, Italy, just across the street from George MacDonald's house, and it whispers a tale of Scotland and the North Wind and my family's journey south to Italy from the forested Swiss Alps.

To my right, on the little wooden table beside my chair, sits a black, leather-bound Bible with my name embossed on the lower right of the cover. The many pages within carry a trans-lation of the Word of God, the Word that told trees to exist in the first place, and those words are made alive by a holy wind blowing through the book's leaves. That living Word planted a seed in my parents, a seed that fell on good soil, and they in turn planted in me and my siblings an imagination-grounding story about a tree in a garden, a tree on a hill of death, and a tree in a heavenly city. Those trees fill my heart and my head, and they keep my compass trained on the Kingdom. Here in the Chapter House, at the dark edge of Warren Wood, the trees keep me company, and they keep me warm.

I am kept by trees.

The garden outside my window is dormant, not dead, because I know tulips and hyacinth, daffodil and crocus bulbs are already crowning out of the mulch, patiently practicing resurrection. There's a tangible energy in the brown, brittle ruins of last year's cottage garden, because I have seen that patch of earth renewed by spring, and spring has begun its inexorable advent. I know it's coming, and my body yearns for it. When my footsteps crunch on the pea gravel path as I make my way under the arch and back to the house, my mind tingles with the image of what the garden was, and what it will be again. I have worked it, on hot days and cold, stacking stones and spreading compost, weeding and planting, laboring to bring order from this wildness in order to make something of the world where God has planted me and my wife. This garden keeps me awake to the necessity of hope, and it keeps me humble because there is no end to the learning, nor the labor.

I am kept by this garden.

The full moon rises over the hill behind The Warren, gleaming through the tall fingers of hackberry and elm and casting its cool light across the field where the old, stout white oaks slumber in the gales, to the valley where Mill Creek quietly glides over flat slabs of limestone. From the front porch I turn to look out on the misty, moonlit bulk of the distant hillside where the valley rises beyond the water, and I know the developers have their eye on all those arbored acres. They see it as a way to make cash, but I want them to make community. I pray once again that whoever buys that land cares more about the next hundred years than the next quarterly report. Let them build something good and beautiful, something that will enfold these diverse families into the loveliness of Cane Ridge rather than driving them further apart by short-sighted, unimaginative, and inhospitable blight of more and more subdivisions with nowhere to walk to. We need more than houses; we need homes, in places we can love. Oh, Lord, let them build something that makes Cane Ridge a *place*, where it's easy to love this creek, to walk these vales, to know these glorious humans who live and move and have their being here. I hope to see the Kingdom on earth as it is in heaven, even in the way we plan our streets and footpaths and communities. It's a long shot, but I keep hoping.

I am kept by hope.

I turn from the blustery night and step inside, gently closing the front door because I know Jamie's sleeping. The kids are all grown now, so it's just the two of us. I begin the routine of shutting down the house: brushing my teeth while I move from door to door, making sure everything's locked up tight, flipping off light switches as I go, making sure the firescreen is closed. I turn out the last light and stand there in the dark, toothbrush in hand, appreciating the red, crackling heartglow of embers that were invisible till now. Trees, spending themselves to keep this house (and my cold-natured wife) warm. I'm certain I'm not the first to pause this way, delighting in the elemental beauty of a hearth fire illuminating the deep dark of a sleeping house.

Reluctantly, I turn away to rinse my toothbrush before climbing into bed. As I drift to sleep, I pray for my children, my extended family, my friends. Some nights it's hard to believe in much of anything. But on nights like this I feel the warmth of my sleeping bride, hear the occasional pop from the fire in the other room as the wind howls in the eaves, and I feel his goodness and his gaze. He's there and listening. The sound of the distant train blast as it rumbles through Antioch, following the berm beside Mill Creek, tugs my attention to the night beyond the window, and to the moon and the wind and the barking of dogs. I feel again the quiet patience of catmint, snowdrop, yarrow, and aster roots in the garden, just ten yards from my bed, blossoms waiting in the exile of winter for spring to fling open the gate to Eden again.

With each successive moment, by the unfolding of time, Christ's creative Word continues its pronouncement that he is King of it all. The Word keeps speaking, and the universe whirls on. If he stopped, we wouldn't know it because there wouldn't be anything left of us to know. But his love keeps pronouncing spring, articulating childbirth, enunciating thunderheads, reciting nectar flow like a poem, conducting the orchestra of time from one movement to the next—trees clapping their hands, myrtles bursting into flower, grapes swelling on the vine, the earth tilting enough to darken the northern hemisphere and ignite the maple leaves, snowflakes piling precariously on the backs of high twigs, sequoias shooting skyward and fattening like balloons—all because Jesus said so. He keeps the whole thing going, holds it all together because he loves us. Love is his glory, and his glory is our joy. He keeps the story going till its magnificent end. Until then he keeps the ache blooming in our chests with every hammer blow of beauty, keeps us hungry for the wedding feast with every eucharist, every gathering of the saints. Even in pain, death, and danger, he keeps our ending safe as houses in the promise that the sorrow now is a countermelody to the impending trumpet blast of joy.

Sinking into sleep, I allow my mind to drift over our little house, up into the rush of wind that rakes the treetops, where I can see the moonlight gleaming on the silver strand of the creek wending its way between the darkling hills, all the way to the Cumberland River. Up and up I go, through the last of the atmosphere, till I see the receding earth in all its sorrow and splendor, then beyond the solar system and the wild, whirling galaxies, until at last I imagine myself crashing through the walls of the universe, where Time and Space are held like a book in the hands of Jesus. He shows me the ending, with a gleam in his eye.

"Behold, I'm making all things new."

I wake, and it's morning, and the sun has crested the hill and cast its yellow beams on the stone arch. I rise again to work and keep this garden, for I am kept by love.

AFTERWORD

Assuming you're reading a printed version of this book (and I hope you are), you're holding in your hands something made out of trees. This is the fruit of a year of work, not to mention the many years of the trees—maybe those at the paper mill near my parents' house in Lake Butler?—growing from seedlings to tall, skinny pines ripe unto their papery harvest, and indeed I hope these chapters will bear their own fruit in you.

At the very least, I hope this book helps you to see how wonderful trees are. That's it. They're all around us and easy to overlook, but they were made by God to be either good for fruit or simply pretty to look at. Right there in Genesis 1, God made trees and validated beauty for beauty's sake. Take the time to allow your eyes to be pleased by their drooping branches and shaggy trunks, their white petals in springtime and their blaze in autumn. This is a pure gift, straight from the mind of Jesus. Next time you eat an apple or a pecan, taste and see that the Lord is good. When you go on a hike, keep your eyes peeled for the oldest trees. Learn their names. Stop to touch the bark. Reckon with their agelessness and remember that they were here before you were. It's a safe bet that they'll outlast you, too. Treat them accordingly.

Second, I hope that you'll keep in mind that trees bear witness. When it comes to doing the hard work of remembrance, we don't have much to go on. Most of our memories up and vanish, and the time line of what we do remember is sure to get discombobulated as we age. But trees give us a place to hang our hats. Think hard about the trees you remember, and if you're anything like me, they'll turn out to be sage and gentle keepers of your days, unlocking memories long since forgotten. Like Abraham, you may even meet the Lord there.

Third, no matter what you do for a living, find a way to get your hands dirty. Most of us have access to a few square feet of dirt. Learn to grow something. Gardening is an embodiment of hope. You may think of it as a hobby for old people and tree huggers, but that's just not true. In a literal sense, it's at the core of what we were made to do and to be. If, like me, you struggle with some measure of depression or melancholia, I'm convinced that it's good medicine.

Fourth, as the title of the Jane Jacobs essay, "Cities Are for People," suggests, the very earth was made for people. This world belongs to the Lord, and if you're a Christian, you belong to him, too. We have a mandate to take care of the place, and we're told in Scripture that the master of the house is returning. This is more than an environmental concern (though it is certainly that, too). It extends to the way we build things, the way we get around, the way we do the business of life. If God intends for us to flourish, we disregard the flourishing of his creation at our peril. Infrastructure, city planning, creation care, justice, neighborliness, and stewardship of resources are all theological concerns.

Most of all, I hope you'll find in my story enough of your own that you, too, can dare to believe that Jesus is God, and he loves you. If you're one of those kids lingering at the back of the crowd, afraid to approach that gentle Jewish rabbi for a blessing, don't be afraid. He loves you. Let him love you.

The temple of God is the place where earth and heaven meet. This is true of Jesus, who called himself the temple— and by the indwelling of his Holy Spirit, it is now true of us. Every child of God rambling around the neighborhood is a temple, a confluence of earth and heaven, a tree whose earth-bound roots drink from the river of God and whose branches breathe his heavens. A wedding day is coming when the New Jerusalem will descend, we'll see the face of our True King, and we will at last know the fullness of time and place and, above all, love. Let us live in the surety of that love by working and keeping what is within our reach, for the good of his creation and the glory of his name.

Dig deep. Branch out. Bear fruit.

ACKNOWLEDGMENTS

At the beginning of the dreaded year 2020 I committed to writing this book without a clear sense of what it would be. All I knew was that I couldn't play music and I had a book deadline. A small group of writers who were in various stages of their own projects agreed to get together weekly, not for critique but for encouragement and conversation. (When you're trying to write, it helps if once in a while you actually feel like a writer.) Thanks to my brother A. S. "Pete" Peterson, Jonathan Rogers, Randall Goodgame, Doug McKelvey, Jennifer Trafton, Russ Ramsey, and Steve Guthrie for listening to my rambling ideas about trees and giving me the guts to write this book. Jonathan and Pete read an early draft and then gave me the guts to cut the chapter I worked hardest on, which of course made the book better by a long shot. (When you're trying to write, it helps if once in a while you act like an editor.) William Thomas Okie, a professor, author, and tree expert in Georgia, got wind of the fact that I was working on a tree book and shot me an email, pointing me to some really helpful resources. He graciously read an early draft and helped me to see what this book was really about. Thanks, Tom, for that great kindness. This book wouldn't exist without Tim Mackie, Jon Collins, and the amazing team at the Bible Project (www.bibleproject.com), who dedicated ten episodes of their podcast to the significance of trees in Scripture. Many thanks to my editor Devin Maddox and the team at B&H for giving me a great excuse to think about trees for a year. It's a great gift to work with such a generous team. Stephen Crotts is one of my favorite artists/

antique banjo players in the world, and it's an honor to have yet another of his works grace the cover. Thanks, Stephen, for perfectly capturing our front garden at The Warren, and for changing the goldfinch to a wren—a wren I like to think has returned after a long winter to nest in the hollow of an oak. Thanks to Christie Bragg for more than two decades of partnership. I showed my son Aedan how to draw when he was ten, and he's been my teacher ever since. Thanks, laddie. One day I'll be half as good as you. The Warren wouldn't be what it is without Aedan, Asher, and Skye's childhoods filling the trees with laughter, stories, and peace. They've proved to their old man that it's possible in this life to be known and loved. Finally, thanks to Jamie, my bride, for twenty-six years of encouragement, affection, and patience.

ABOUT THE AUTHOR

Andrew Peterson is an award-winning singer-songwriter and author. The second book in his series The Wingfeather Saga, *North! Or Be Eaten* (2009), won the Christy Award for Young Adult Fiction, and the fourth, *The Warden and the Wolf King* (2014), won World Magazine's Children's Book of the Year in August 2015. Season one of *The Wingfeather Saga* animated series is currently in production.

In 2008, driven by a desire to cultivate a strong Christian arts community, Andrew founded a ministry called The Rabbit Room, which led to a yearly conference, countless concerts and symposiums, and Rabbit Room Press, which has published thirty books to date.

He's been married for twenty-six years to his wife, Jamie, with whom they have three children. His eldest is an illustrator and animator, his second son is a touring drummer and record producer, and his daughter recently released her first album. In his spare time Andrew keeps bees, builds dry stack stone walls, gardens, draws, and sleeps.

ALSO BY THE AUTHOR

Books

The Wingfeather Saga

Book One: *On the Edge of the Dark Sea of Darkness*

Book Two: *North! Or Be Eaten*

Book Three: *The Monster in the Hollows*

Book Four: *The Warden and the Wolf King*

Wingfeather Tales, ed.

Pembrick's Creaturepedia

The Ballad of Matthew's Begats

Music

Carried Along

Clear to Venus

Love & Thunder

Behold the Lamb of God

The Far Country

Slugs & Bugs & Lullabies (with Randall Goodgame)

Resurrection Letters, Vol. 2

Counting Stars

Above These City Lights

Light for the Lost Boy

After All These Years: A Collection

The Burning Edge of Dawn

Resurrection Letters: Prologue

Resurrection Letters, Vol. 1

Adventure is Waiting . . .
Discover the Bestselling and Award-Winning
Wingfeather Saga by Andrew Peterson